THIS I CAN BELIEVE

THIS I CAN
BELIEVE

*An Outline of Essentials
of the Christian Faith*

BY
ALFRED GRANT WALTON

WITH A FOREWORD BY
COLONEL HUGH L. COOPER

Essay Index Reprint Series

BOOKS FOR LIBRARIES PRESS
FREEPORT, NEW YORK

INTERNATIONAL STANDARD BOOK NUMBER:
0-8369-2207-7

LIBRARY OF CONGRESS CATALOG CARD NUMBER:
79-142708

PRINTED IN THE UNITED STATES OF AMERICA

CONTENTS

Foreword

IF ANY group of ten successful men and women were separately to make a list of the major qualifications contributing mostly to the successes which they have achieved, the word "faith" would undoubtedly be found at the top, or near the top, of most of these lists. The group might give varying definitions for the meaning of this term, but the sum of all the definitions would be the certain principles or truths on which they could absolutely rely, and of which they could say, with positive assurance, "This I can believe." Search the records of human achievement as thoroughly as we can, and as far back as recorded history permits, and we find that one of the outstanding gifts to man is the power created by belief. Faith asserts itself most clearly in the presence of great difficulty, indeed it seems to shrink the difficulty and helps to overcome the obstacles that hinder the realization of our purposes. Thus faith leads to progress and achievement, while doubt leads to discouragement and despair. We need it now. An intelligent analysis of the world's present social, political, and economic diseases will show that one major

cause for our trouble is a lack of confidence in our
governments, our leaders, and in ourselves. Edna
St. Vincent Millay summed up the might of faith
when she wrote:

> Faith it is
> That keeps the world alive. If all at once
> Faith were to slacken—that unconscious faith
> Which must, I know, yet be the corner stone
> Of all believing—birds now flying fearless
> Across, would drop in terror to the earth,
> Fishes would drown; and the all governing reins
> Would tangle in the frantic hands of God
> And the worlds gallop headlong to destruction.

Just as the capacity for faith is exercised in
problems related to our material welfare, so it
must be employed in any spiritual effort. We
need, as a basis for the religious life, some convictions in which we may absolutely trust. If the
component parts are not bound together and supported by faith, religion will achieve nothing, as
history has clearly demonstrated. Unfortunately,
many in the past and in the present have been dull
pupils. We learn our lessons with majestic slow-
ness and are prone to forget that which has been
taught us out of life's bitter experiences. In these
present days there is an insistent demand for re-

newed reliance not only on our own inherent
capacities but on spiritual values as well. As we
look at the situation created by the depression we
recognize that the Great War had much to do
with the difficulties which now surround us, and
we reasonably decide that one of the outstanding
forces necessary to rescue us is a return of confidence. This is true, but that restoration of confidence is required coincidently in the affairs of
the material world and in our moral and religious
ideals. Only by the assertion of such a faith will
men attain their rational stature and meet the circumstances now confronting the world.

In all scientific progress related to our material
welfare, progress has come through the lessons
learned in the school called "Trial and Error."
Graduates from this institution have had much
to do with all the achievements of civilization. By
this method Truth is discovered and fallacy is cast
aside. Religion should follow the same course. We
should seek those fundamental beliefs which best
interpret life and all human experience. Those
who have been willing to apply the teachings of
the school of "Trial and Error" in religion have
emerged with a faith stronger than ever before.

The Bible stands out to-day, after centuries of

study, as the best guide for men and women to follow for their spiritual determinations. The practical teachings of the Bible have remained unchanged, and do not need changing for the guidance of correct living. Along the material highway the guide posts have been so constantly shifted that we have often lost our way. In this respect, the history of material progress has lacked the certainties which Christianity has possessed.

Therefore, the task is clearly set before us to discover the basis for a rational and intelligent faith through a proper understanding of the Bible, and thus to gain the dynamic force so greatly needed in the modern world. It seems to me that this book, *This I Can Believe,* helping as it surely will to a better understanding of our all-important spiritual life, will be broadly welcomed at this particular time.

HUGH L. COOPER

Preface

THE modern man wants some religious ideas in
which he may fully believe. The lack of interest
in organized Christianity, which has been observed in recent times and which has given church
leaders much concern, is an attitude neither
rooted in indifference nor founded upon contempt. It is partially the result of a certain confusion of thought arising from a vague sense of
uncertainty regarding what is true and what is
false, and from a consciousness of a difference between the teachings of yesterday and to-day.

The man of to-day has a pathetic eagerness for
spiritual reality—as deep and as earnest as any
displayed in the past—but often he is unable to
find it. He is increasingly aware that some of the
ideas taught him in childhood, and to which he
gave unhesitating assent, are no longer tenable.
His religious thought has been affected by the
scientific spirit which has characterized his time,
and he is disposed to raise questions and to examine the authoritarian declarations of the past. No
longer is it sufficient that some religious position
has the support of the creeds or the approval of

the church. He is willing to respect both of these witnesses, but he realizes that the only Truth valuable for him is that which he himself can believe is true. The final seat of authority is in his own heart. Of course, religion will always be more than the rational mind can formulate, but in so far as it is presented at all, it must be compatible with common sense and do no violence to one's highest intelligence.

But certain practical difficulties face the ordinary man who is seeking a well-balanced and satisfying conception of religion. The commonplace demands of his life forbid extensive studies in the field of Christian thought such as theologians are able to pursue. The necessities of earning his daily bread, of fulfilling social responsibilities and of meeting the multifarious demands which go with the business of living, leave little time for specialized studies. In so far as he is able to read any of the works of accredited theologians, he is hampered by a lack of proper historical background and by an unfamiliarity with many of the technical terms involved, so that he does not get far upon his way.

This book is for such a person. There is a living, vital faith in which the alert, intelligent man of the modern world may believe; a religious faith that does no violence to the broad witness of human experience in other fields of study, and of which one need not be ashamed. The author has sought to answer some of the practical inquiries which arise in many minds, and to present briefly and succinctly the great essentials of the Christian religion in language that can be clearly understood. He has envisaged the church member in the Sunday congregation, the business man in his office, the woman in the home, the clerk at his desk, the critical young student returning from college, in fact all who come in the category of the average citizen. To this average man—who is the hope of America and the church—he has addressed himself in the preparation of these pages.

It is hardly to be expected that the reader will accept every position set forth in this book, nor is it important that he should do so. Christianity is a way of life, and is therefore infinitely more than any intellectual formulations about it. But the contemplation of important questions is bound to be helpful to any individual who, with reverent heart and open mind, is unafraid to consider the full meaning of the Christian faith.

In no sense can the material be considered original. The author has drawn freely on the researches of eminent scholars and gratefully acknowledges his indebtedness to them. He is simply a torch-bearer passing on to others a light kindled at greater fires than his own.

Special acknowledgment is made of the kindness of Col. Hugh L. Cooper in writing the "Foreword." Colonel Cooper's accomplishments in the water power projects at Niagara Falls, N. Y., Keokuk, Iowa, Muscle Shoals, Alabama, and more recently in the construction of the great Dneiper dam in Russia have given him a preëminence as one of the world's greatest hydro-electric engineers. His emphasis on the value of faith and the importance of religion is of noteworthy significance, coming as it does from a professional man and a layman of outstanding distinction.

The author is indebted to Charles Scribner's Sons, Publishers, for permission to quote from *The Crystal* in *Poems by Sidney Lanier*.

A. G. W.

Tompkins Avenue Congregational Church,
Brooklyn, N. Y.

THIS I CAN BELIEVE

CHAPTER I

How Did the Bible Originate?

THE great Book of the Christian faith quickens and inspires all who come into contact with it. Its pages are filled with soul-stirring messages that stimulate the intellect, arouse the emotions, and give a mighty impulse to the moral will. The writers were acquainted with God. One cannot read the lofty utterances of the prophets, the beautiful songs of the Psalmists, the wise admonitions of the apostles, or the sublime teachings of Jesus without a consciousness that the Bible is unique in the literature of the world. The reverent reader finds his heart aglow as he is lifted into the realm of the spirit, shares the visions of the religious seer and discovers the good counsels of those who knew God.

The Bible is our chief source of information regarding Jesus Christ and his teachings, a fact which in itself is of outstanding significance, since the literature of the world offers nothing comparable to his insights into the realm of religion and morals. Humanity has had other interpreters of the religious life, like Confucius and Gautama, who spoke many words of wisdom and laid the foundations for mighty religious systems, but none has ever reached the pure levels of spiritual discernment attained by the Oracle of Galilee. He spoke from the mountain top of exalted vision, and the truth which he brought to the world finds a quick response in the consciousness of thoughtful men.

It is remarkable that a single book could have exerted such a far-reaching influence on human history. Yet there is a certain inaccuracy in thinking of the Bible as one volume. In reality it is a library, or compendium of many books, bound together. Some of them were written centuries before Christ was born. Others were inscribed many decades after his resurrection. The entire scope of the Bible covers a period of nearly two thousand years. Any thoughtful reader will discover that the books comprising the Old and New Testaments could not have been written at one time, and they represent an accumulation of religious literature extending through many generations.

The fixed and authoritative group of books

recognized by the Christian Church as sacred
Scripture is called the "canon." The meaning of
this term should be clearly in our mind. The word
originated in the Greek and meant a reed, a pole,
or a measuring rod. We get the idea when we
think of any piece of wood used for measuring
purposes, such as a carpenter's rule or a yardstick.
Gradually, by the principle of metonymy, the
word came to mean a rule or standard by which
anything might be judged. The canon of the
church denotes the general teaching of the church
which was accepted as the standard or norm by
the Christian fellowship. By degrees the meaning
of the word "canon" changed even more, and it
was finally used to indicate the group of books
received by the Church as sacred Scripture, and
which, as such, became the standard of truth
and conduct. This idea was definitely established
by 350 A. D., and at that time the word took on the
meaning associated with it to-day. The canon is
now conceived as a definitely determined and
authoritative list of books which are considered as
sacred Writings. The catalogue of accepted list-
ings has remained the same in recent centuries,
and will never be changed.

The Jews surrounded the books which they considered as Scripture with the idea of holiness. The messages were holy, and therefore the written rolls on which they were inscribed were holy. These documents were handled with the greatest care and with much reverence. In connection with this idea of holiness, a peculiar expression developed, namely: "The Book defiles the hands." The hands had to be washed with pure water after contact with holiness, because holiness was contagious, and if one were to touch an unholy thing with hands made holy through contact with holiness, he would be guilty of bringing holiness and unholiness together. When ancient writers used the expression, "The Book defiles the hands," we know that the writing so described had reached canonical rank, and was held in high veneration. This unusual phrase has been very helpful in determining the date when various documents reached the stage where the honor belonging to accepted Writings was given to them.

Since the Bible did not spring into being, fullgrown and complete, it is necessary for us to study the various steps by which it assumed its present form, and only in so doing can we have an adequate understanding of the Book itself.

The Old Testament Canon

The examination of the earliest available manuscripts of the Hebrew Bible make it clear that the books were divided into three groups. These groups are as follows:

  (a) The Law, or Torah:—Genesis, Exodus, Leviticus, Numbers and Deuteronomy.

  (b) Prophetic Books:
    (1) The former Prophets: — Joshua, Judges, Samuel, I and II Kings.
    (2) The later Prophets:—Isaiah, Jeremiah, Ezekiel, and the minor Prophets: Hosea, Joel, Amos, Obadiah, Jonah, Micah, Nahum, Habakkuk, Zephaniah, Haggai, Zechariah, Malachi.

  (c) Sacred Writings:—Hagiographa.
    (1) Poetical Books: Psalms, Proverbs, Job. Rolls: Song of Songs, Ruth, Lamentations, Ecclesiastes, and Esther.
    (2) Miscellaneous:—Daniel, Ezra, Nehemiah, and I and II Chronicles.

There is very strong evidence that this three-fold division stood out clearly in Jewish minds. We find the suggestion of it in Luke 24:44. There is also a reference to this tri-partite division in an old book called Ecclesiasticus, or the Wisdom of Jesus, the son of Sirach, which is now found in the Apocrypha. This book may be dated 190-170 B. C., and in the prologue, written by the grandson of the author about 132 B. C., the division of the Old Testament books into three parts is clearly indicated. One may wonder why our present Bibles do not follow this arangement of the books. The explanation is to be found in the preference of Christian scholars for the ancient order of the Alexandrian Jews, who translated the Jewish Scriptures into Greek. It is in the Alexandrian translation that we find the classification of books under a four-fold grouping of Law, History, Poetry and Prophecy, such as we have in our Old Testament today.

There must have been a time when there were no writings considered sacred by the Jews. But early in the life of these deeply religious people there appeared a great mass of literature containing poems, anecdotes, historical records and prophetic utterances which were highly cherished. There were also old collections of laws dealing with Jehovah's relations to men. One of the oldest of these compilations was the Ten Commandments. Some of this literature, although never attaining canonical rank in the Old Testament, was held in great esteem. One might mention the Book of Jashar, to which reference is made in Joshua 10:12-15, and the History of Samuel, the Seer, spoken of in I Chronicles 29:29.

Before there could be any canon of sacred Scripture, there must have been a community of believers who had developed sufficiently in their religious life to believe that it was possible for God to reveal His divine will through literature.

The First Recognition of Holy Writings

The first recognition of any writing that was considered holy was in 621 B. C., in the eighteenth year of Josiah, the king. Some repairs were being made in the Temple, and while the work was going on, the high priest, Hilkiah, discovered a small book which he realized to be of great importance. He reported the matter to the king, through Shapan the scribe (II Kings 22:10). When the king heard the book read, he was disturbed because of the idolatrous practices of the people and "because our fathers have not hearkened unto the word of this book, to do according unto all that which is written concerning us." A great assemblage was called, and the king instituted sweeping reforms. He made a covenant before Jehovah "to walk after Jehovah and to keep his commandments, and his testimonies, and his statutes with all his heart, and all his soul, to confirm the words of this covenant that were written in this book" (II Kings, 23:3) . This little volume, which was the first to attain the rank of sacred Scripture, was not the same as our five books of the Law, but was a part of our present book of Deuteronomy. During the next two centuries this book was combined with earlier laws and some later priestly legislation. The oldest collection was the Ten Commandments (Exodus 20:1-17) ; still another group of laws was known as the Book of the Covenant (Exodus 20:20 - 23:33) . It is not known exactly when the compilation of this material occurred, but possibly some of it was done while the Jews were in exile in Babylon. We do know that in 457 B. C., at the time Ezra returned with a great company of Jews to help restore the city of Jerusalem, they brought with them the book of the Law of Moses.

One evidence that these writings were considered as canonical in the fifth cenutury B. C. is found in the schism which occurred among the Jews in Jerusalem.

Manasseh, a priest who was driven out of the temple, went to Mt. Gerizim, where he established a rival temple of worship. The worshippers on Mt. Gerizim were the Samaritans, who were greatly despised by the Jews, even in Jesus' day. The Samaritans adopted for their sacred Scripture books which Manasseh had taken with him. These writings so closely resembled the books of the Law that there is no doubt of their relation to each other. Manasseh took all the canonical Scriptures of the Jews which were accepted at that time. Had other writings been raised to this important rank it is quite certain he would have taken them too.

In all the writings after the exile, the Law is assumed to be a final authority. It was read and copied with the utmost care. We get an idea of the veneration which was shown toward these books in the practice of the Alexandrian Jews among whom the Law had to be given to the people in Greek. Seven persons were chosen to read the text. Three verses were read by each person, the eyes had to be kept on the text while being

read, and only one verse at a time could be given
to the interpreter.

The Prophets

During this period in which the books of the
Law were being raised to a position of canonical
importance, there were other books of religious
literature written by the prophets which were
greatly respected. These writings differed from
the Law in that they were addressed to the particular times and the prevailing conditions during
which the prophet gave his message. There was
frequent controversy regarding true prophets and
false prophets, and by 333 B. C. it was believed
that prophecy had died out. Josephus, the great
Jewish historian, states that no books after Ar-
taxerxes, 425 B. C., were inspired, because there
were no prophets after that time.

By 200 B. C. the books of Prophets were well
established as sacred Writings. They were accepted
as such because the Jews had found them full of
hope and used them frequently. In the days of
the persecutions by Antiochus Epiphanes, the
ruler of Syria, who tried to destroy the worship
of Jehovah, it was natural that the devout Jews
should wish to preserve their messages of comfort

and promise. It is very clear that at the time the prologue to the book of Ecclesiasticus was written (about 132 B. C.), this second group of writings was received as Scripture.

The Other Writings

Of course, there were still other religious books which were held in high veneration and were considered of deep spiritual value, even though they did not come from the pen of the Prophets. They have been called the Hagiographa, or the Other Writings. The Book of Psalms, and Job are in this group. Some of this third collection were accepted as books which "defile the hands" by certain groups and rejected by others. Among the books in our present canon about which there were particular disputes were Ecclesiastes, Esther, and the Song of Solomon. On the other hand, the book of Ecclesiasticus, or the Wisdom of Jesus, was popular in many places, but was finally rejected. Esther was disputed because the name of God did not appear in it. Ecclesiastes was questioned because some of its statements seemed heretical. First and Second Maccabees were quite popular because they dealt with the dramatic story of the trying Maccabean period. The books which comprised this third group were not finally accepted until long after the birth of Christ, although some of them individually attained canonical rank before the beginning of the Christian era.

The Close of the Canon

Toward the end of the first Christian century, a number of factors conspired to close the Jewish canon of Scripture. The Temple at Jerusalem had been destroyed in 70 A. D. as a result of the vicious and devastating attack of Titus. In the final capitulation of the noble city one of the soldiers of that Roman emperor cast a burning firebrand into the Temple, and that holy edifice was destroyed. From that date the Jews had no place which they could call home, and no rallying point for the religious life of their people. With the removal of the firm bonds holding the faithful together, it was highly desirable that the question of the canonicity of the various books, about which endless discussion had been carried on, should be settled once and for all.

Again, the Greek translation of books, called the Septuagint, was becoming very popular. It was used more in Palestine than the Hebrew writ-

ings, since pure Hebrew, which had given place
to Aramaic, a dialect of the Semitic language,
could not be read by many. Greek was the common language of the times. The Septuagint contained a number of books which the Palestinian
Jews did not care to accept, and there was a fear
among the religious leaders that if a definite Hebrew canon were not soon determined, the Septuagint would be accepted. As the Septuagint was
not in the original Hebrew, but was simply a
translation, there was a deep concern lest the pure
word of Yahweh might be distorted before reaching the people, and an erroneous and inaccurate
form of the Hebrew scriptures thus become established.

But there was still another reason for the close
of the canon, far more important than those already given. Christianity had begun to make its
influence felt in the world. The earnest disciples
of Jesus were preaching everywhere and winning
new converts to their faith. In furnishing proof
for their religious contentions, they often dared to
quote from some of the Christian writings, perhaps an epistle of Paul or one of the Gospels,
using exactly the same expressions that were com-

mon when one quoted Scripture. In other words, the Christians also were beginning to think of some of their writings as holy. In the face of all these conditions it was felt that something should be done to settle the question regarding the disputed books, and to fix the Hebrew canon once and for all. If this were accomplished, the Jews throughout the world would have a common group of sacred writings which would be accepted everywhere. There would be no chance for other books than those sanctioned by the Palestinian Jews to get into the canon. Christian writings would be definitely excluded.

Accordingly, a synod was held some time between 90 and 100 A. D. in a little town called Jamnia, on the border of Judah, not far from Joppa. The religious leaders of the people were there. They discussed the canonicity of the disputed books and at that synod, by definite vote, the books that are now included in our Old Testament were definitely chosen. It is likely that in some instances the votes were not unanimous. Special emphasis was laid upon the canonicity of the Song of Songs and Ecclesiastes, about which there had been many arguments. They were finally included among the books which "defile the hands." This assembly settled the question of the Hebrew canon. Occasionally protests arose later, but the decision of the synod was accepted as final.

Certain Observations

The formation of the Jewish canon was the result of a gradual process of growth. The Bible of the Jews did not come into existence overnight. God used holy men as His instruments and worked through them in various times and under various conditions to bring His revelations to the world. The Old Testament is a religious deposit of the best thought of the religious leaders of the Hebrew people. The chief factor in determining canonicity was common acceptance and usage, and it was because certain books seemed more helpful than others that they finally attained their prominence. Some of the Old Testament writings are more valuable than others. The human element is present in all of them, and yet, when one reads these hallowed pages, particularly in the light of their historical development, they take on new meaning, and their messages have increased significance.

The Formation of the New Testament

The early Christians considered the Jewish Bible as their own. Jesus used it, as did also his followers. There were certain groups, such as the Ophites and the Marcionites, who repudiated the Old Testament, but it was not so with the main body of Christian believers.

There were a number of factors which delayed the formation of the New Testament canon. First, there was the expectation that Jesus would return soon to the earth in physical form and establish his Kingdom among men. Therefore there was no need for any record of his life. Again, the Christians already had a body of Scripture, and there seemed to be no need for more. Still another reason was the primitive simplicity of the early church. It was comprised of humble people coming, for the most part, from the ranks of manual toilers such as the fishermen and artisans of the day. Only a few could read or write. Parchment or papyrus was expensive, and everything that was written down had to be inscribed laboriously by hand. Such conditions favored an oral rather than a written tradition. An apostle would recall an unusual saying of Jesus, and this would be repeated to others. If Jesus' comments happened to be in paradoxical or unusual form, they could easily be remembered. Such incidents were retold again and again, and in course of time the sayings and anecdotes became definitely fixed, in much the same manner as proverbs or maxims of our own time. It is quite evident that when the Gospels were written there was large dependence upon the accumulations of oral tradition. Under all these conditions, it was quite natural that there was considerable delay before any writings appeared which would be raised to the ranks of hallowed Scripture.

The first of our New Testament writings were the letters of the apostles. The little groups of faithful Christians in Corinth, in Colossae, in Ephesus, and in other parts of the world looked with great satisfaction upon a letter from one of the church leaders. Sometimes these letters would deal with definite problems of the church, such as the excesses that appeared with the newly-found liberties of the Christian faith. The words of admonition, of counsel, and of good cheer in one of these communications would be read frequently. They would be taken from one place to another where some other small community of believers had formed a church, in order that they might also share the inspiration and encouragement. Thus there developed a Christian literature, just as the previous centuries had produced a definitely Jewish literature. Devout followers of Christ wrote down collections of his sayings, incidents and anecdotes about his life, and sermons on Christian themes. In such a group of writings it was to be expected that anything from the pen of an apostle would receive special attention. Likewise, anything dealing with the life of Jesus would be highly prized. Such discriminations were very natural.

The first of our New Testament writings to make an appearance was not the Gospel of St. Matthew, as some might assume, since it happens to be placed first, but the First Epistle of Paul to the Church at Thessalonica. It was written between 48 and 50 A. D. Not long after the appearance of this letter others were sent which were later regarded as canonical. It is quite likely that some of the apostolic letters were lost.

The Gospels

The Gospel of St. Mark, the oldest of the gospel narratives, appeared about thirty-five years after the earthly ministry of Christ was brought to a close (65 A. D.). John Mark was a personal friend of Peter, and secured his information from him. Eusebius, the Church historian, in referring to the writings of a certain Papias, bishop of Hierapolis, who lived in the first part of the second century, states that Papias wrote the following: "This also the presbyter (John) said: 'And Mark, having become the interpreter of Peter, wrote down accurately, though not in order, whatever he remembered of the things said and done by Christ, for he never heard the Lord nor followed him, but afterwards he followed Peter, who adapted his teachings to the needs of his hearers, but with no intention of giving a connected account of his Lord's discourses, so that Mark committed no error while he thus wrote some things as he remembered them, for he was careful of one thing—not to omit any of the things he had heard and not to state any of them falsely.' "

This makes it quite clear that Mark secured his material through Peter, but that his narrative was not intended to be a complete or connected life of our Lord. We can easily understand how such a writing, with such definite apostolic authority, should one day come to be regarded as canonical.

When the gospels of Matthew and Luke were written, the authors had the text of Mark's gospel before them, although they had other source material. Apparently Matthew and Luke had a collection of the sayings of Jesus which Mark did not have. These sayings have been called the Logia, or the words of Jesus. The Gospel of John is a spiritual meditation on Jesus' life, particularly in the light of Greek philosphy.

It was a long time before any of these writings were held as inspired Scripture, but in an old letter called the Epistle of Barnabas, dated between 119 and 126 A. D., we find for the first time a passage from Matthew 22:24 quoted with the customary phrase which the Jews used when writings were considered canonical. From that time on many Christian writings began to be quoted in a similar way. Near the middle of the second century a man named Tatian published a book called the Diatessaron, which was a single narrative embodying the four Gospels, and which showed that these books had then attained great importance. As time went on there is evidence that some books were occasionally quoted as scripture which never were ultimately accepted; for example, the Epistle of Barnabas, the Preaching of Paul and the Gospel according to the Egyptians.

The basis for the selection of the New Testament books as accepted writings was apostolicity. The Gospels were readily included because they had this apostolic authority and contained the narrative of Jesus' life. Some books, like the Epistle to the Hebrews (to name only one), were questioned, because the western churches were not sure who wrote them. The Revelation of St. John was not accepted in the 'Syro-Palestine churches, and so differences of opinion prevailed as in the case of certain of the Old Testament books.

The first list that we have of New Testament books which are regarded as holy Scripture is to be found in a tattered old document known to scholars as the Muratorian Fragment, dated about 170 A. D. Most of our present New Testament books were included, but the Epistle of James, I and II Peter and the Epistle to the Hebrews were left out.

Closing of the New Testament Canon

The New Testament collection of writings took on definiteness toward the close of the second century, and for a number of reasons. First, the development of Gnosticism was an important factor. The Gnostics were a heretical sect, which looked upon Christianity more as a philosophy than a religion. Many of them rejected the Old Testament and repudiated the Christian connection with Judaism, and they accepted only such Christian writings as seemed to conform to their particular notions. The Christians desired particularly to preserve the writings of the apostles which they considered genuine and authentic. Apostolic authorship was determined by agreement of the teaching of the books containing the apostolic traditions and the doctrines preserved by the churches.

Again, the persecutions by Diocletian in 303 A. D. furnished another element helping to fix the New Testament canon. The Christians were hounded by persecution, and if they were found with copies of sacred Writings in their homes the punishment was severe. One would not care to jeopardize his life or his personal comforts by secreting a book which he was not sure was genuine and of real importance.

The first canonical list of the New Testament exactly like our own is found in an Easter letter written in 367 A. D. by Athanasius, archbishop of Alexandria. His list of the Old Testament and New Testament books is exactly like the one which we have to-day. Thirty years later, at a great council held in Carthage, ecclesiastical support was given to the present canon of the New Testament, although the Eastern churches questioned the Revelation of St. John and some of the epistles. It was not until the seventh century, nearly 400 years later, that the East and West came to a common agreement on the canon. Even in Reformation times there was a difference of opinion regarding the New Testament books. It is well remembered that Luther questioned the book of James, calling it an epistle of straw. The Catholic Church, in the famous council of Trent, adopted as its canon of Scripture our present Old Testament and New Testament, and also the apocryphal books.

Basis for Canonicity

In the case of the New Testament, as in the Old, the basis for acceptance was usage, and usage was determined by a belief in apostolic authorship and also upon the intrinsic value of the books themselves. Our Old Testament and New Testament books have come to us through a gradual process of growth, and their selection was finally made as the result of the spiritual values which were found in them. God used many men, with the limitations of their own times upon them, to interpret His truth to others. In accepting the present canon of Scripture we do not repudiate other Jewish or Christian writings as worthless; many of them are helpful, inspiring and worthy of reverent study.

To know the way in which the Bible was formed enhances our veneration for it. This compendium of religious literature is of value for the Truth which it contains. To understand it is to love it, and when one reads it, he is ready to give assent to the judgment of the Jews and the early Christians that this Book contains the eternal word of God. The God who directs the stars in their courses and who has revealed Himself through all the ages in nature, in law, and in human life revealed also His guiding hand and controlling wisdom in giving man this Book of Books.

CHAPTER II

How Was Our English Bible Developed?

THE development of our present English Bible
furnishes a narrative of dramatic interest. It is a
thrilling story of the work of hundreds of scholars
guided by a passionate longing for accuracy and
dominated by a resolute purpose to discover the
Truth. Often they worked in the face of bitter
opposition, at times they were persecuted, and
some even paid the penalty of a martyr's death.
Thousands of fragile manuscripts have been
brought from ancient repositories, their yellow
pages scrutinized with the utmost care and every
possible effort made to give the world an exact
record of the books which comprise the Bible.
Only a deep recognition of the worth of these
revered Writings and the importance of the truth
which they contain could have prompted so many
noble men in every century to give their lives
in painstaking devotion to this sublime task.

The books of the Bible were not originally prepared in the form of books as we now know
them, but were written on rolls, and the work

was done by hand. In the early church these records were called *Ta Biblia,* the Greek words for "The Books." It is from the old word *Biblia* that we have derived the present name for our sacred Writings. The word "Bible" did not appear at the beginning of our books of Scripture until the early part of the sixteenth century, but the use has continued from that time until now. When the writings of the Old Testament were first prepared, it is quite likely that they were inscribed on leather or parchment. New Testament books were generally written on papyrus. This writing material was made from the stem of the papyrus plant, which was cut into thin strips. The ribbons were laid side by side to make a sheet. A second layer was superimposed at right angles to the first, and then the two surfaces were pressed together and held in place by glue. Sheets of this material could be fastened together by gluing the edges, and a long roll of writing material could be produced, or individual sheets could be bound together to form a book. This latter method developed very early, possibly in the first century, and proved very convenient, for a document in book form was more easily handled than the cumbersome rolls. It was not long before this form of preparing the writings of the Bible became very popular.

The Books of the Old Testament

None of the original documents which comprise the Old Testament are in existence. Indeed, the oldest copy we now have of even a part of the Old Testament dates back no farther than 916 A. D. This manuscript contains only the books of the Law. Since one thousand years had elapsed between the completion of the last books of the Old Testament and our oldest existing copies, it is amazing to discover that there are relatively few variations in the text. This is due to the very great veneration which the Jews had for their sacred Writings and the scrupulous care that the copyists exercised in transcribing the words and letters. If some one discovered an obvious error in the text, the mistake would be copied just as it occurred and the correction would be placed in the margin. In doing the work of transcription even the size and shape of letters were reproduced, and lines were arranged to come out exactly as they were in the document from which the writer worked.

A special group of men known as Massoretes

gave themselves to this particular task. They considered it their solemn duty to pass on the Scriptures in exact conformity to the established traditions of the Jewish people. They worked with unusual care, even counting words and letters so that none would be omitted. Ancient Hebrew writings did not include the use of vowels, and later these were indicated by marks or points placed below, between, or above the consonants. The Massoretes assumed the responsibility for providing the Hebrew Scriptures with the vowel marks. The oldest dated manuscript of the Hebrew, containing only the books of the Law, has vowel points placed in the three different positions. This important document, referred to previously, was written about 916 A. D. and is now in the British Museum.

It is thought that the Jews adopted a standard text for their sacred books at the beginning of the second century and that variations from this standard were destroyed. As a result of the painstaking efforts of the Massoretes, who were specialists in their field, and also because of the process of standardization, old Hebrew copies of the books of the Old Testament were very uniform and relatively free from textual errors.

A Greek Translation—The Septuagint

The Jews endured great hardship and suffering in their native land, and wars and persecution caused many of them to move elsewhere. A large colony settled in the great city of Alexandria, in Egypt. This thriving metropolis was Greek in language and customs, and the Jews who chose to live there naturally adopted the Greek tongue as the language most convenient for their use. Soon the Palestinian families neglected their mother tongue and, before many generations had come and gone, a large number of them were unable to speak Hebrew at all. But the loss of their language did not mean a lack of interest in national traditions or in their own religion. These pious people desired to preserve the sacred Law and the great prophetic utterances of their race. Therefore, a translation of the Jewish scriptures into Greek was started in 275 B. C., but over one hundred and fifty years elapsed before the task was completed. This Greek translation is known to scholars as the *Septuagint*.

An interesting legend regarding the *Septuagint* is worthy of repetition. The reigning Pharaoh is said to have sent representatives to Palestine to search out devout and learned men who knew the Greek and Hebrew languages. In due time they brought back seventy-two scholars to carry out the important work of translation. They were given an elaborate banquet, after which each one went to an individual room, where he worked for seventy-two days on the translation. When these men emerged from their confinement, their work was compared and the translations were found to be absolutely identical. Because the number of scholars was approximately seventy, the Greek translation of the Old Testament was called the *Septuagint*. The story is undoubtedly false, and yet it suggests the high regard in which this translation was held by those who used it.

The *Septuagint* contained not only the books of our present Old Testament but also the so-called apocryphal books, with the exception of II Esdras. This famous work found wide acceptance not only in Egypt but among Greek-speaking Jews throughout the world. Jesus and his followers used it, as is clearly indicated in some of the Old Testament quotations from his lips. Many more translations were made from it into other languages, and even to-day there are some

Eastern churches that follow the Septuagint as the official text of the Old Testament.

The Books of the New Testament

Just as in the case with the Old Testament writings, none of the original New Testament writings are extant. These books were written originally in Greek. An extensive search has been made for old copies since, naturally, the older documents are particularly valuable. Two types of writings were used in the earliest manuscripts. These are called uncials and cursives. Uncials were usually written on vellum. Capital letters were used, words were run together and some abbreviations were followed. This type may be dated between the fourth and ninth centuries. The cursives were written in a flowing hand more like writing as we use it today. This style could be produced more rapidly than the uncials, the letters did not have to be shaped so carefully, and they did not occupy so much space. The uncial period extended from the ninth to the fifteenth centuries.

It is quite evident that in the first two centuries of the Christian era, when the books of the New Testament had not reached the high level of veneration which they have attained to-day, copyists felt free to insert new material into the original texts which had come into their hands and which they felt brought additional information or added clarity to the text. One illustration may suffice. In Luke 9:55 it is recorded that Jesus rebuked James and John for asking that fire from heaven be sent down to destroy those who had refused hospitality to him. The copyist, who evidently felt that Jesus' attitude was stern, sought to temper his words by an additional statement which may or may not have been made in connection with this particular incident. At any rate, we have the additional comment: "Ye know not what manner of spirit ye are of, for the Son of Man came not to destroy men's lives but to save them." Certainly the spirit of this phrase harmonizes with the spirit of Jesus and it would not be strange if he actually expressed it. The beautiful incident recorded in John 7:53-8:11, in which Jesus showed compassion on a woman who had committed adultery, was not a part of the original text and is so indicated in our modern Bibles. Yet it is true to the temper and spirit of Jesus and seems a worthy and authentic tradition.

There are three famous uncial manuscripts

which are the prized possession of the church today and with which we should be familiar because of their great antiquity and their important textual value.

The Vatican Manuscript—Codex Vaticanus

This manuscript receives its name from the library of the Vatican in Rome, where it may be found. It is one of the oldest New Testament manuscripts in existence. When Constantine was emperor of Rome he had fifty Bibles prepared for him by expert copyists, and this codex is thought to be one of them. It contains all the characteristics of an uncial. The letters are capitals, there are no divisions between the words, and there are abbreviations of words like God and Jesus, evidently made to save time and space. Only in recent years has the *Codex Vaticanus* been made available for scholars. At first the Catholic church guarded it sedulously, but in 1890 photostatic copies of each page were produced, and now the scholars of the world may study it freely.

The Sinaitic Manuscript—Codex Sinaiticus

This manuscript was found in the monastery of St. Catherine, located at the foot of Mount

Sinai, and from that well known Biblical place it has received its name. The discovery of this famous uncial may be credited to a talented German scholar by the name of Lobegott von Tischendorf. He had a special interest in manuscripts and in his peregrinations he chanced to visit this monastery. It was in the year 1844. While looking around he happened to see a basket containing some old sheets, in the great hall where the monks were accustomed to congregate. His scrutiny of them revealed that the pages were written in Greek, that they contained parts of the Old Testament and were of great antiquity. He took forty-three of these sheets and left for his own country. Nine years later he went back in search for more. This trip was unsuccessful, but coming again five years afterwards, this time with credentials from the Tsar of Russia, who had a spiritual protectorate over the monastery, he hoped for better results. He found a few interesting documents but none of special value. On the very night before he had decided to leave he happened to take a walk in the garden with one of the monks, who later invited him to his cell for refreshments. While eating together, the robed ecclesiastic remarked casually that he had a copy of the Scriptures. Thereupon he took down from a shelf an old volume wrapped in cloth and spread it out before Tischendorf. Here were not only the fragments he had taken from the basket years before, but other parts of the Old Testament, the New Testament in its entirety, and part of the apocryphal writings. The trained German scholar was aware that he had run across one of the most valuable manuscripts in existence. Later the monks were induced to present the manuscript to the Tsar, and for many years it was in the library at St. Petersburg. The present Soviet government, having no interest in the Christian religion, recently sold this codex to the British government for the amazing sum of $510,000. This amount of money could have purchased a library of between 100,000 and 200,000 books, yet this fabulous price was gladly paid for these old pages, yellow with age and fragile with the ravages of years. *Codex Sinaiticus* is dated about the fourth century.

The Alexandrian Manuscript—Codex Alexandrinus

This manuscript follows the Alexandrian canon of the *Septuagint* and also contains most of the New Testament. Two books known as the Epistles of Clement are included in the Christian writings. The writing of this manuscript indicates a date of about 425 A. D. *Codex Alexandrinus* was given to Charles I, king of England in 1628. It may be found today in the British Museum in London.

The Vulgate

A proper understanding of the development of the English Bible demands some knowledge of a famous Latin translation which exerted a far-reaching influence on subsequent efforts to bring the Scriptures to men. It is called the *Vulgate,* which means "currently received," and the books which comprised it were the ones which were currently accepted at the time. It included our present Old and New Testaments, and the Apocrypha. The author of this scholarly work was a man known as Jerome, a priest of the fourth century. He was a prominent ecclesiastic and was at one time secretary to Pope Damascus, in which position he exerted a powerful influence. When he reached middle life he moved to Jerusalem, where he became the head of a monastery and where he had ample opportunity to follow his scholastic interests. Pope Damascus recognized in Jerome a man of outstanding abilities and one of the truly great scholars of his day, and when he decided that there was a need for a good translation of the Bible into the Latin language he turned to this man to carry out the important enterprise.

Jerome took his assignment seriously and spent many years at his arduous task. In the preparation of the Old Testament, he worked from the original Hebrew and from the *Septuagint,* and in transcribing the New Testament he used Greek manuscripts and an old Latin version. Jerome lived a hectic life, finding himself in frequent theological controversy, not only with heretical sects, but even with the Church itself, which did not fully appreciate what he had accomplished in its behalf. It was not until long after he was dead that he was given just honors for his years of devoted labor. The *Vulgate* came to be one of the truly great landmarks of Biblical development. For centuries it was used by other translators in the English and other languages, and the Catholic Bible of the present day is based upon it.

The English Bible

It was inevitable that the time should come when the Bible would find its way into the English language, and it is with the progress of that development that we are mostly concerned. The steps were slow and gradual, the way was beset with many difficulties, and some of the consecrated men who made the final result possible met persecution in the way. First, reference should be made to an English rustic of the seventh century, named Caedmon. Not a great deal is known about him, but according to such information as is available, he had a dream one night, while sleeping in a stable, that God commanded him to go forth and sing of created things. In obedience to this mandate, he went about chanting fragmentary anecdotes from the Bible, in the vernacular of the people. This was the first real step in the long process of bringing the treasures of the Bible to the masses.

From time to time different individuals translated portions of the Old and New Testaments, but it remained for John Wycliffe to be the first person to put all the Bible into the English language. In this important undertaking he had the valuable assistance of a certain Nicholas Hereford. Wycliffe was a reformer, and while in Oxford he attracted much attention by his pronounced views on religion. He organized a group of wandering preachers, who went from place to place bearing the Christian evangel to the common people. When he was sixty years of age he brought forth a translation of the New Testament in his mother tongue, and followed it two years later with a translation of the Old Testament as well. For his source material Wycliffe used the Latin *Vulgate*.

This gifted scholar had the laudable purpose of making the great truths of the Bible available for all his fellow countrymen but, like many others who have been actuated by high motives, he was severely criticized for what he had done. The bitterness of the opposition toward him is revealed in the contemptuous remark of one critic, who said of him: "He has made the Bible more common and open to all laymen and women than it was wont to be to clerks of good education and understanding, so that the pearl of the Gospel is cast underneath the feet of swine!" Even death did not calm the opposition; not only were his Bibles burned or destroyed, but four decades after he had been laid to rest his bones were disinterred and his ashes scattered on the little stream near his church at Lutterworth. His associate, John Purvey, also had a hard time of it, was cast into prison and probably died there.

But time moves on, and two centuries later another brilliant light appeared in the firmament of England's religious life. This was William Tyndale, who was also interested in Biblical translation for the people of his native land. The authorities were not so sympathetic to such activities as was Tyndale himself, and he found it necessary to go to Germany for his work. His New Testament was finished in 1525, and in its preparation he relied largely on the *Vulgate,* as Wycliffe had done before him. Tyndale also translated parts of the Old Testament into English, basing his labors on Hebrew manuscripts. In order to avoid trouble, he had his Bibles printed abroad, and they were then smuggled into England. This was necessary since the Church did not favor giving the common people access to the sacred Books. Despite his lofty purposes, Tyndale was persecuted almost continuously; his life was constantly threatened, and as a final reward for his monumental endeavors, he was imprisoned for fifteen months and then burned at the stake. No one has exerted so large an influence on our present English Bible as this man. Both the King James version and the American Standard Bible have borrowed copiously from his work.

The first English Bible in which each verse was paragraphed and the books were divided into chapters is called the Geneva Bible. William Whittingham was largely responsible for its appearance. He belonged to a group of scholars who fled from England to escape persecution and made their home in Geneva, from whence this Bible derived its name. It was finished in 1560, had a popular reception and ran into one hundred and forty editions.

The Roman Catholic church had never been kindly disposed toward an English translation of the Bible, preferring to keep the great Book in the hands of the Church, to be interpreted by it to the people. But the time came when an English translation became virtually imperative for the members of that faith, and so a group of Catholic scholars in the Seminary at Rheims embarked on the important undertaking. Jerome's *Vulgate*, which others had used so freely, furnished the basis for their scholastic labors also. When disputed points arose, a Catholic rendition of them was printed in the margin. The New Testament was finished in 1582 and the Old Testament in 1610. The names of William Allen and Richard Bristow are outstanding among those who labored in the production of this Bible. The Seminary at Rheims was moved later to Douai and consequently this translation is called the Rheims-Douai Bible.

The King James Version—the Authorized Version

In 1604, at the request of the Puritans, King James of England prepared to translate the Bible into English. For this important task he selected a group of fifty-four scholars from the ranks of the clergy and laity. In following this policy, the translation which was ultimately produced and carried his name was distinctive in that it represented the labors of many scholars rather than a few, as in the case of previous translations. This body of men applied themselves assiduously to their task for over two years and nine months, and then they gave their work to the world. It was dedicated to the King, under whose auspices they had worked. The King James Version is striking for its dignity and elegance of language, for its beauty of expression and for a certain noble simplicity. Even to-day it is, for many people, the most satisfactory form of our sacred Writings.

The Revised Version

The King James Version proved very acceptable for over 200 years, but gradually there came a demand for another translation of the Bible into the English language. A number of reasons contributed to this development. The knowledge of the Greek texts had increased immeasurably, and the three most famous manuscripts, the Vatican, Sinaitic and Alexandrian, had become available for research. The men who produced the King James version did not have this valuable material for their work. There had also been considerable change in the use of many English words, so that the King James Version did not always convey the exact thought which was intended. Some two hundred words were found which had changed their meaning or had become obsolete.

The British revision came as a result of a recommendation of a committee of the English Church that asked that such a work be attempted. Fifty-two representatives from England participated in the actual translation, as well as an advisory committee of twenty-seven from America. Their labors extended from 1870 until 1885. When the British revision was finally completed there was a distinct improvement in the text, and chapter and verse divisions were subordinated to paragraph distinction. Likewise, the poetry was printed in a different manner than the prose.

The American Standard Bible

The American Committee which had collaborated with the British group to produce the Revised Version agreed not to bring out a Bible of their own for fourteen years, but they did continue their work, and ultimately produced an American Standard Bible which was given to the world in 1901. It is a very superior translation. Throughout this Bible the word "Jehovah" has been used to indicate God. Some improvements were made in translation. This version used "Sheol" to indicate the abode of the dead rather than the erroneous translation of the word as "hell" or "pit" in the Authorized Version. Some offensive words in the King James Version were likewise changed in the interest of elegance. The American Standard Bible stands today as one of

the most accurate translations of the inspired
Writings in existence.

Modern Translations

A number of scholars have translated the Bible
into modern speech. Among them are Richard F.
Weymouth, James Moffatt, Edgar J. Goodspeed,
and William G. Ballantine. These private translations have been done with much care and with
full consideration of all available material. They
are stimulating in their thought, clarifying in
their language, and helpful for a better understanding of the Bible, but they will probably
never replace the Authorized Version or the
American Standard Bible, both of which represent the combined scholarship of many persons.

Interesting Facts Regarding Translation

One is able to get a fair idea of the tremendous
amount of work involved in bringing the Bible to
its present form by knowledge of the many documents that had to be considered in the preparation of the text. There are one hundred and
fourteen codices from the fourth to the tenth centuries, and approximately twelve hundred other
manuscripts dating from the ninth to the six-

teenth centuries. All of these were made by hand and offered the human possibilities of error. While no one can tell exactly the numerical variations in the texts, it has been pointed out that in the case of the New Testament there are nearly 150,000 of them. Of this great number, not more than fifty really affect the thought and, even in these cases, other passages from the Bible are sufficiently clear on the points involved so that there is no necessity for misunderstanding or alarm.

Some of the ancient copies of the Scripture contain curious errors, and Dr. P. Marion Simms, in his book *The Bible from the Beginning*, has given an elaborate list of them. In Jerome's translation of Exodus 34:35 the Hebrew for the phrase "Moses' face shone," was translated erroneously by the phrase "Moses' face was horned." Michelangelo's statue of Moses was horned on the forehead, and apparently this idea was the result of Jerome's faulty translation. The Geneva Bible published in 1560 is also called the "Breeches Bible," because the translation of Genesis 3:7 states that Adam and Eve "sewed fig leaves together and made themselves breeches." The socalled "wicked Bible" of 1631, which was a copy of the Authorized Version, translated Exodus 20:14

as "Thou shalt commit adultery" instead of "Thou shalt not commit adultery." A severe penalty was imposed upon the printer for this mistake. One Bible came to be known as the "Bug" Bible, because it translated Psalm 91:5 as "Thou shalt not need to be afraid for any bugs by night" instead of "Thou shalt not be afraid for any terror by night." Coverdale's Bible, published in 1535, contained this odd translation.

Conclusion

The Bible which we have to-day is the result of scholarly efforts extending over hundreds of years. Though every original Bible manuscript is lost, we may feel certain that our American Standard Bible is about as exact a translation of the original documents as though they were extant. Evidently men have found the Bible of sufficient value to justify this long and arduous study. They have become convinced that in this Book is to be found the eternal Truth of God, and with a passion to discover that Truth they have carried on their studies exhaustively. Through their devoted labors we have a priceless possession, the modern English Bible, in which may be found the eternal Word of God and a clear portrayal of His will for man.

CHAPTER III

What Shall We Believe about the Bible?

THE preëminence of the Bible is unquestioned in
the field of literature and in the realm of morals.
Abundant testimony of its artistic excellence has
been offered by scholars who are able to appraise
aesthetic values. The King James Version, with
its chaste and beautiful selection of words, its simple and dignified sentences, its clear and concise
statements, is one of the finest examples of literary
expression in the English language. The moral supremacy of the Bible is attested by the wide influence it has exerted in the life of the world. The
Christian church has based its teachings on this
noble Book, and history has revealed intellectual,
social and moral progress wherever Christianity
has gone. The Bible will never be displaced, nor
will it lose its prestige as "the Book of Books."
Storms of controversy have raged about it, ene-
mies of religion have endeavored to undermine
its foundations, critics have sought to destroy it
but, like a lighthouse built upon a rock, it has remained strong and enduring through the centu-

ries, casting its benign light over the sea of human life.

Yet the Bible has suffered greatly at the hands of its friends. Christians have found this book so helpful and inspiring that often exaggerated statements have been made going far beyond anything which this Book claims for itself or which may be substantiated by the facts themselves. There is always a disposition toward over-statement of that which appeals most to us. But the object of our devotion may suffer if false and unreasonable affirmations are made which cannot be justified, and earnest seekers after Truth, who might otherwise come under the helpful influence of the Bible, may turn from it altogether if it is not fairly and honestly presented to them.

Any study of the Bible should be carried on reverently and sympathetically. Any Book which has brought inspiration, comfort and light to countless thousands of men and women is deserving of such consideration whether we are willing to accept it or not. We should study the writings of Confucius or the teachings of the Koran in a similar manner. Our opinions regarding the Bible should be the result of our own studies and observations. No one should be expected to accept the

theories of others or the pronouncement of ecclesiastical councils held centuries ago unless they can
be verified in personal experience. The only way
to an appreciation of art is through absolute honesty with ourselves, and we have no right to insist
that the Venus de Milo or the Mona Lisa are
beautiful because art critics have pronounced
them so. They are beautiful when we ourselves
have discovered the secret of their charm. So, too,
the value of the Bible must be discovered by each
individual through earnest and reverent study.

No book has ever been written about which
there have been so many divergent opinions as the
Bible, and this despite the fact that no book has
been more seriously studied. These differences
have existed through the centuries, and the dis-
agreements of traditionalism and liberalism are
by no means confined to our own time. There has
not even been unanimity of opinion among religious believers regarding the exact books which
constitute the Bible. The Jews claim only the Old
Testament. The Samaritans acknowledge only the
books of the Law. Protestant Christians accept the
Old Testament and the New Testament, while
Roman Catholics use these and the so-called apoc-

ryphal books. Under these circumstances every man must do his own thinking.

There are two claims which have been made about the Bible which have been brought seriously into question and which have furnished the basis for many contentions. These are the assertions that the Bible is verbally inerrant and that it is infallible. It is well for us to consider both of them.

Is the Bible Verbally Inerrant?

When we speak of the verbal inerrancy of the Bible we mean that every word in it is without error, exactly as it was originally written or as the message was first spoken. Absolute honesty to the facts make it clear that we cannot hold to such a position. Not one of the original manuscripts is now in existence. The Bible that we have now is a translation from documents written centuries after the original books were inscribed. These ancient records were copied from others which preceded them. When one contemplates mentally the mechanical difficulties of transcription by hand he realizes the many possibilities of error. The oldest copies of Old Testament and New Testament books show many variations with each other.

What is more, our English Bible is a translation into an entirely different language from the original Hebrew and Greek, and the meaning of words can never be absolutely taken over from one language to another. We have many different English translations, and if we were to defend verbal inerrancy, we would have to determine which one of these compendiums is the correct one. Is it Moffatt's translation or the American Standard Bible, or the Authorized Version? All of these English Bibles give excellent translations but none can lay claim to verbal inerrancy.

Further proof against the presumption of this idea comes from the internal evidence of the Bible itself. An illustration from the New Testament will make this point clear. In each of the four Gospels the author records the superscription placed upon the cross of Jesus, and in each case the words are different. The four inscriptions which have been given are as follows:

Matthew 27:37	"This is Jesus, the King of the Jews."
Mark 15:26	"The King of the Jews."
Luke 23:38	"This is the King of the Jews."
John 19:19	"Jesus of Nazareth, the King of the Jews."

The record of the Sermon on the Mount is given in two places in the Gospels: in Matthew 5-6-7, and in Luke 6. These two transcriptions of that memorable discourse of Jesus are not identical in material or in words. A comparison of the Beatitudes in these passages offers an interesting field for research. If any one will take the time to make careful studies of other parts of the Gospels he will find abundant justification for the position that, however valuable the Bible may be, it is inaccurate and unfair to claim that it is a verbally inerrant book.

Is the Bible Infallible?

Infallibility is a more inclusive term than verbal inerrancy. It conveys the idea of freedom not only from verbal error but also mistakes in statement of facts, historical data and moral teaching. If the Bible is infallible there can be no contradictions in it, no historical inaccuracies and no variations in its moral teachings, and every part will harmonize with every other part. This is asking a good deal of so many different books, written by many authors over a period of more than a thousand years, but such must be the case if this claim is to be maintained. But what does a study of the

Book reveal? An examination of a few unusual passages will be illuminating.

In the Creation narrative in the book of Genesis we read: "And Jehovah God said unto the serpent: 'Upon thy belly shalt thou go and dust shalt thou eat all the days of thy life' " (Genesis 3:14). Here is a scientific inaccuracy. Serpents do move without the use of pedal appendages but they do not eat dust! Leviticus 11:21-22 contains a statement of dietary regulation among the Jews: "Yet these may ye eat of all winged creeping things that go upon all *fours* which have legs above their feet; even these of them ye may eat, the locust after its kind, and the cricket after its kind, and the grasshopper after its kind." This is curious, for locusts, crickets and grasshoppers have six feet and not four! Even if it were asserted that the kinds of insects to which reference is made were not the same as the ones which we now know by these names, our translation would then be inaccurate, and that is contrary to infallibility.

A curious contradiction in the book of II Samuel may be cited to show another type of error. II Samuel 6:23 states "Michal the daughter of Saul had no child unto the day of her death." Later in this same book, II Samuel 21:8 refers to

"the five sons of Michal the daughter of Saul."
Here we have two statements that are directly opposite to each other. A similar contradiction is
found in the Acts of the Apostles and is related to
Paul's vision on the road to Damascus. Acts 9:7
reads "And the men that journeyed with him
(Paul) stood speechless hearing the voice, but be-
holding no man." Paul, in describing his experience in Acts 22:9, asserts: "They that were with
me beheld indeed the light but they heard not the
voice of Him that spake to me." While these incidents deal with facts which are trivial and unim-
portant in themselves, they make it clear that a
study of the text itself contradicts any claim of
historic infallibility.

There are also some moral teachings in the
Bible that are quite irreconcilable with others in
the same Book. Deuteronomy 21:18-21, gives it as
God's command that a rebellious son shall be
stoned to death, and yet God's commandment
given to Moses on Mount Sinai is "Thou shalt not
kill." Exodus 22:18 says "Thou shalt not suffer
a sorceress to live." This passage furnished justification for many deaths in the persecution of
witchcraft and is wholly out of harmony with
other teachings in the Bible. The Imprecatory

Psalms, such as Psalms 69 and 109, reveal a spirit of vindictiveness and hatred contrary to the whole spirit of Jesus and his conception of a loving and a forgiving Father.

The insistence on verbal inerrancy and infallibility may not seem of great consequence to many students of the Bible, and certainly the illustrations which have been cited are not of sufficient importance to lessen one's appreciation of the value or importance of the Bible itself. Yet these ideas may be very dangerous because, if they are once accepted, they lead to interpretations of the various books that end in great confusion. Such false claims about the Bible lead to the practice of quoting individual verses out of their context to support some prophetic idea and they also support the so-called "proof text" method in the exposition of the Scriptures, a system which can furnish Biblical justification for almost any theological whim that one may fancy.

The Proof Text Method

The proof-text method is based upon the assumption that the Bible is an organic whole, that all parts harmonize with each other, that there are no mistakes. Therefore, texts may be selected from

various parts of the Bible and joined together indiscriminately. There are groups of Christians
looking for Christ's imminent return to earth in
visible form in the present day, and they support
their position by indiscriminate quotations from
the Gospels, the Book of Daniel, and the Apoca-
lypse. Yet the writers of these Books were different
men, working at different times, under wholly different circumstances, and dealing with entirely
different situations. The conservative who be-
lieves in the doctrine of salvation through blood
atonement establishes a very good argument for
his position by a joint citation from the Old
Testament writings dealing with the blood sacrifice of the Jews, and by passages from the Epistles
of Paul. Seventh-Day Adventists justify their contention that Saturday and not Sunday should be
celebrated as the day of worship by passages from
the Old Testament Law and the record of Jesus
as found in the New Testament. Almost any
theory or doctrine can be bolstered up if one may
join individual verses together like pearls upon a
string, to establish a contention. Many of the
strange religious sects of today support their positions by the proof-text method.

The proof-text method also permits individual

verses to be wrested from their context in order
to support ideas that are in no way related to the
situations with which the verses deal. One writer
asserts that automobiles are prophesied in Nahum
2:4 because he finds there: "The chariots shall
rage in the streets, they shall jostle one another in
the broad ways. They shall seem like torches, they
shall run like the lightnings." Mormons, premil-
lenarians, believers in the gifts of tongues and
many others feel that the Bible fully substantiates
their positions and they invariably use this false
method to prove their point.

To appreciate the meaning of any text in the
Bible it must be considered in the light of its context, with full consideration to the circumstances
and conditions under which the words were written. To link verses together indiscriminately is to
make the Bible a book of magic, and almost any
theological vagary can be justified in this manner.
There is real foundation for the truth in the old
adage that even "the devil can cite Scripture for
his purpose."

Is the Bible a Historical or Scientific Book?

The Bible should not be considered as a book
of history. Of course, there are records of histori-

cal events in both the Old and New Testaments, but the historical motive is never the dominant one. In so far as there are historical records, they should not be appraised by the standards which we use today. The modern historian collects his data from a wide range of sources. He carefully compiles and checks his materials in every possible way. He seeks to weigh his facts carefully, and to give each one its due measure of importance. He aims at absolute accuracy of fact, and seeks proper historical sequence. These motives are not to be found in the books which comprise our sacred Scriptures.

When we examine the record of Jesus' life in the Gospels, we find that it is very fragmentary. Except for one or two passing references, the first thirty years in the life of our Lord are ignored completely. These were important, eventful years which must have been very significant in shaping the plastic, growing mind of this pious young man. No true historian would have ignored them. When we come to the public ministry of our Lord, there is no unanimity of opinion among the gospel narrators regarding the correct sequence of events. What we have are really collections of scattered incidents and events in the earthly life of

Jesus arranged in the historical continuity which
seemed reasonable to writers who did their work
thirty or forty years after Christ's earthly career
was over. In the ancient writings of Papias to
which reference was made in a previous chapter, it
was noted that Mark wrote accurately, but *not in
order*, the things which he had received from
Peter.

Who can contemplate the wealth of teaching
which Jesus uttered, and the noble deeds of mercy
and love which were overlooked and have been
lost to the world forever? The Evangelists wrote
for different groups and with different purposes
in mind. Matthew sought to convince the Jews
that Jesus was the Messiah. Mark wrote especially
for the Roman Christians, and Luke apparently
had Greek readers in mind.

Nor should the Bible be studied as a scientific
book for, when the books were compiled, science,
as we know it to-day, was unknown. The development of the scientific spirit is a product of recent
years, and the religious writers who produced the
Bible knew nothing about astronomy, evolution
or natural law. The story of Creation in the book
of Genesis is altogether contradictory to the overwhelming evidence that the earth and all that is

on it developed as the result of a laborious process extending through countless ages. We must be as ready to read what God has written in the book of Nature as we are to read what he has revealed in the sacred pages of our Holy Book.

It is impossible to believe that God shaped a man out of dust and actually breathed into his nostrils to make him live. Who can accept the idea that woman was made from a rib of a man, that a serpent talked to Adam and Eve in some unknown language and that the whole process of creation was completed in a single week? All our studies in embryology, physiology, geology and astronomy rise up to protest against such a claim. The Creation story represents simply a pious and reverent attempt made long ago to explain the riddle of creation. It shows rare insight in its insistence upon one God, and not many gods, in its emphasis on a gradual process of growth, and in its high moral content. It is far superior to other Creation legends of the time, with which it has some parallels, but it is not scientifically accurate.

When the Psalms were written it was thought that the earth was flat, that the sky was supported by gigantic pillars which held a canopy, above which were waters, occasionally leaking through in the form of rain. Such conceptions seemed reasonable when these great hymns were written, but we know to-day that they are not true. These primitive people also believed in dragons and unicorns, they felt that diseases were caused by evil spirits and that the heart and not the brain was the center of thought and of the emotional life. Any attempt to make the Bible a scientific book is sure to lead us into trouble.

The Bible—A Record of Progressive Religious Experience

The chief interest of Biblical writers was neither historical nor scientific, but religious. The Bible is primarily a record of religious experience on the part of a very religious people. Just as Rome gave law to the world and Greece gave philosophy, the Jews made their chief contribution in the field of religion. This race was the most religious that the world has known. They were convinced that there was a God who ruled their lives and directed their destiny. They sought to understand Him and to know His will and purposes for men. They felt that they were His chosen people through whom His truth was to be given to the world.

The writers of the books of the Bible were human beings like ourselves. They were limited by the thought forms and beliefs of their times. They had to deal with definite political and social situations. They spoke out of life's real experiences. They were the spiritual seers of the world's most religious people. What we have in the Bible is consequently the loftiest spiritual insights of the greatest religious souls of the world's most religious people.

The truth of God which these men brought to the world did not come into existence full grown, as did Minerva from the brow of Jupiter, but was given through a slow and gradual process—a progressive revelation which found its culmination in the life and the teachings of the noblest soul that ever walked the earth, the historic Jesus of Nazareth. The writers felt themselves in full fellowship with the Lord of all creation and did not hesitate to declare boldly: "Thus saith Jehovah." As we read their words, compare them with our own experiences, study them in the light of the religious aspirations of other noble souls, we become convinced that here in this great repository of Jewish laws, history, poetry, proverbs and homily is the very truth of the eternal God.

When we consider the Bible as a progressive record of religious experience, we are freed from all the difficulties which are created by the erroneous theories of the past. Many college trained men and women have turned from the Bible because it has been presented to them in a way that is completely at variance with their historical and scientific studies. But one can accept every contribution of science and every advanced conception of philosophy and still find in the Bible that wisdom and truth from God which the soul craves in its search for spiritual reality. We may believe in this great Book. It is deserving of veneration above all others, and if anyone will take its sublime religious truths and make them a part of his life, he will find his soul moving along that straight and narrow highway that leads to the throne of God.

Inspiration and Revelation

The Bible is an inspired Book, but in making such a statement regarding it we should have clearly in our minds what "inspiration" means. Inspiration is a certain quickening or heightening of spiritual experience as the result of some new knowledge, illumination or truth which has come

home to the soul. When we read the Twenty-third
Psalm, the majestic prophecies of Isaiah and
Amos, or the high priestly prayer of Christ (John
17), we are lifted to high levels of emotional response and insight. These are inspired writings,
and the true test of inspiration is found in its effect upon us. Some inspiration is greater than
others. Amos inspires us more than Malachi. The
Psalms quicken us more than the book of Nehe-
miah. While any writer of the Bible may have
been inspired when he gave his message to the
world, the value of his inspiration to others is dependent upon the ability of his message to produce a similar emotional and intellectual response
in us.

Revelation should not be confused with inspiration. Revelation has to do with the impartation of
God's thought and message to man. It is because
of the revelation of God to the writers of the Bible
that we find much of inspiration in them. Yet a
message might be a revelation from God reflect-
ing His thought and purpose in certain historical
situations in the past, and yet might be inspiring
only for the contemporary times in which the
Book was written and not for men to-day. If a pas-

sage from the Bible quickens and inspires us, kindles our religious feelings and makes us inwardly aware that we are sharing the everlasting Truth of God, we have a right to say that it is inspired, but that inspiration is not something that exists *per se*, but is the result of what we ourselves have received from it.

The Unity of the Bible

There are some who feel that the Bible is an organic unity, to be treated virtually as though it were a single composition written by the hand of God. This conception has not only led to the fallacious error of the proof-text method in the use of the Scriptures, but it also requires a tremendous amount of intellectual gymnastics in order to adjust its positions. If we remember that the Bible is composed of sixty-six different books, each separate and distinct from the other, and that these are bound together in one volume simply that we may use them more conveniently, we will easily realize the error in the thought of organic unity.

Yet there is a unity which belongs to the Bible, and which deserves recognition. The books are united in dealing with the common subject of religion. They are one in the sense that all of them have been raised to the level of holy Writings, and consequently have been clothed with veneration and influence. They are also one in bringing conviction of the goodness of God, and of his compelling and saving power.

Has the Bible Authority?

The Bible does have an authority, but it is not something that is imposed from without. The American people have made the Constitution the supreme law of the land, and if a man were to commit treason the authority placed in the Constitution would permit his punishment. A similar authority goes with all our statutes. But the authority of the Bible is not imparted to it by some official decree. It is the authority which is regnant and imperial in the nature of Truth itself. This arises from the spiritual supremacy of the Bible and its inner revelation of divine Truth. When a man becomes convinced that he is in the presence of the truth of God—and the Bible brings that conviction—then that authority is the same as the command of God Himself.

Is the Bible the Same as Any Other Book?

The Bible can hardly be considered the same as any other book, for while its authors were not different from other men who have written about religion, their messages represent a loftier insight and a broader influence than can be found in any other literature of the world. The Bible has been the guide, the solace and the inspiration of millions in their search for spiritual reality. It has been the foundation on which the Church has been reared, the greatest institution of virtue that humanity has known. Judged by its effect on human lives, and its influence upon human history, it is absolutely unique in the literature of the world. There never has been, and never will be, another Book like it, because it is a supreme and satisfying interpretation of God's will and purpose for man.

CHAPTER IV

Is There a Personal God?

THE trend of modern thought, with its emphasis on scientific knowledge and its freedom from the restraints of tradition, has brought the reality of God seriously into question. Devout persons, who have heretofore accepted a belief in a Supreme Being with complete confidence, have had their faith shaken by the insistent voices of those who have asserted that the cosmos is a vast machine devoid of all spiritual content and utterly lacking in moral significance. Brilliant writers possessed of persuasive powers of expression have dismissed God jauntily from the universe, and have portrayed Him as a fatuous creation of the mind wholly unworthy of serious consideration. Keen scientists have joined the attack and, looking askance at any disposition to give credence to faith, have stressed the importance of restricting belief to the realm of the wholly demonstrable. Yet the religious man does not easily surrender his most prized possession, nor willingly part with his noblest hope, and devout seekers after Truth continue to search diligently for the evidence which supports their great religious conviction.

The idea of God is the noblest of all Christian conceptions and the inevitable end of all questions dealing with ultimate reality. These interrogations are inescapable, since the rational mind insists upon a reasonable interpretation of all the facts of experience. The final conclusions have far reaching significance, for our judgment about God has a bearing upon our estimate of ourselves, our appraisal of the value of others and the meaning of everything else in life. Is man an insignificant organism living a momentary existence on a minute globule of dust in an infinite and staggering universe, or is he a divine being of eternal worth? Is our neighbor some one whose life we may disregard, whose feelings we do not need to consider and whose interests may be pushed ruthlessly aside, or is he a soul of infinite value? The demands of duty, the value of sacrifice, and the judgments of ultimate destiny are all closely linked to our thought about God.

This explains why this subject is of perennial interest, not only to speculative thinkers and students in academic institutions, but also to the man on the street. Philosophers return to it again and

again. The so-called "bull sessions" in college dor-
mitories are enlivened by its consideration. Any
scientist who is willing to step outside his own
field long enough to express an opinion regarding
God commands immediate attention. The human
mind is so constituted that it persists unwearyingly
in its search for ultimate Truth.

Three Attitudes of Mind

There are three reactions which people have to
the idea of God. Some persons have an assurance
of His reality that is tantamount to absolute certainty, and their faith brooks no denial. They consider that God's existence is a self-evident fact
which, like the maxims of mathematics or the tru-
isms of daily experience, demands no proof. They
point out with positive candor that we need no
reasoned arguments to assure us of our own existence, for although the world and all that is in it
may be a dream, a figment of the imagination, we
know that we exist. We demand no syllogism to
convince us of the reality of the physical universe,
for it impinges on our senses continually. We need
no logic to demonstrate parental love. In like
manner these believers assert the reality of God,
whose presence they feel continually and whose

manifestations are everywhere about them. Their highest and best moments witness to His nearness in the universe. The stars are His diadem, the clouds His flowing garments, the evening zephyrs His gentle voice. He is in the onward march of history, in the trend of human events, in the altruistic deeds of noble souls. Whatever reaction we may have to the convictions of this confident group, we are compelled by an inner integrity to acknowledge that their faith gives serenity and poise to their lives, courage to their moral endeavor and a certain noble dignity to their conduct.

A second group, greatly in the minority, hold a directly antipodal position for they are equally sure that there is no God. For them the idea is a vain superstition, the projection of a fatuous hope, the result of "wishful thinking." They repudiate God completely and hold that such a foolish notion intimidates man and enslaves his thought. Carlyle reflected this gloomy attitude of mind at one time in his life and wrote pessimistically: "The universe is devoid of all life and purpose, of volition, even hostility. It is one huge, dead, immense steam engine rolling on in its dead indifference to grind me limb from limb. O the vast gloomy Golgotha and mill of Death." Among the modern opponents of the God-idea are the members of the American Association for the Advancement of Atheism, a vigorous, militant organization with an extensive propaganda. Similarly, many college professors openly flaunt atheistic ideas, and a large number of their students follow them.

The third group constitutes the majority. They are those who would like to believe in God and who feel a wistful yearning in their hearts for a discovery of Him, but who lack a sense of confident assurance. They are frankly agnostic, and while they would not toss God into the discard, their faith is not sufficient to carry them further than the simple assertion: "We do not know." A distinguished preacher writes in one of his recent books of a young university graduate who told him that he was all at sea regarding God, that his friends were largely in the same condition and that only recently they had talked all night about God and immortality, but in the end they were still at sea.

In whatever group we may find it necessary to classify ourselves, it will be helpful to our thought if we remember that God is incapable of absolute proof, such as one might find in the solution of a problem in mathematics or in the completion of a laboratory experiment. The idea of God encompasses all reality, and is linked up with our understanding of the Absolute, and to know such a God completely would require omniscience, a capacity which man does not possess. But if we cannot prove God we may seek to discover Him.

Reasons for a Belief in God—The Mystery of the Universe

When one looks at the universe to understand it and discover its meaning, he is overwhelmed by its intricacy and its mystery. With all our scientific knowledge which has made startling advances during the last century, and with all the products of philosophical thought by the great thinkers of history, we have comprehended only an infinitesimal fragment of ultimate reality. We deal with laws which we cannot change, force which we cannot control and life which we cannot bring into being. The mere spread of the physical universe staggers the imagination which seeks to comprehend its reality. Such a cosmos, magnificent in its scope, tantalizing in its secrets, creates a sense of reverence and awe within us as we are terrified by its power or subdued by its mystery. But the mind is led in its very wanderings to a conviction that there is reality back of these feelings, a something which we cannot quite grasp but which we are sure exists, and which causes these feelings to arise within us. Professor Otto has designated this as a "numinous" or divine element which has always existed and which has expressed itself concretely in the religions and creeds of man. In the presence of life's unsolved mysteries and out of the hush of eternal wonder comes a demand for a living God.

The First Cause

Likewise, a belief in God asserts itself when man seeks a first Cause. The stellar world with its bewildering immensity is continually yielding new wonders to the astronomers seeking to understand it. Heavenly bodies have been found which are thousands of "light years" from us. Sir Arthur Eddington has said that when we view a certain faint patch of light in Andromeda we are looking back nine hundred thousand years into the past. How did such a cosmos come into being and how did this fleck of star dust which we call the earth, with its marvelous beauty and its varying complexity, assume its present form? Science has also made notable progress in the realm of the infinitesimal, but when it has gone back to its utmost limits in ions or energy, it has nothing to offer regarding origins. When we have travelled through the age-long processes of evolution, back to the sun from whence this earth came forth and then back to the cosmic trend that brought that blazing orb into being, we come face to face with a profound mystery—the First Cause. We cannot imagine a beginning without a Cause, and it is that first Cause which intelligence demands we associate with God.

The Presence of Life in the Universe

Again, this universe calls for an explanation of that pulsating thing known as Life. We are not certain when life first appeared on this planet, but we do know that, when it did appear, it manifested a very unusual capacity—the ability to continue itself in the organisms in which it appeared. So great a biologist as Professor J. S. Haldane has pointed out that this characteristic cannot possibly be explained on any basis of physical or chemical causation. The first forms of animation must have been lowly indeed, probably simple unicellular creations which perpetuated themselves by asexual reproduction, but through the millennia of the years increasingly complex forms developed until the whole world was teeming with living organisms. At last appeared the apex and crown of the whole creative trend—Man himself. Who can explain man with his marvelous mental powers, capable of producing the dramas of a Shakespeare, able to evolve an Einstein's theory of relativity and powerful enough to subdue the gargantuan forces of nature and make them subservient to his will? The whole scheme of Reality reveals a life process moving on continually in the reproduction and perpetuation of organisms, in the changing elements of evolution and in the unfolding processes of the human mind. What Bergson suggests by his *elan vital* the common man associates with his idea of God, and in that Life which permeates his world he finds evidence for an eternal spiritual Reality.

The Element of Rationality

The natural world reveals an element of rationality in its make-up which corresponds to the rational aspects of man's own being. Science has evolved systems of observed phenomena known as laws which are the product of the human mind as it has dealt with the facts of experience. When a man reads a book or studies a musical composition there is a strong presumption that there is something in common between the intelligence that created the book or the music and the intelligence which understands it. We are constantly reading the book of nature, and every discovered law is a passage from it. The physicist splits the atom into protons and electrons, but when he seeks to explain these divisions he does so by mathematical symbols and formulae. This trend in modern science carries a strong presumption that Mind and not matter constitutes the ultimate reality, and the universe speaks of a creative Mind Energy back of all things. No matter what field of natural science engages our attention, we never escape the operation of law, always rational, always reliable and intelligible. It is inconceivable that the universe just happened that way and that our present world is the accidental resultant of force impinging upon matter. Such a notion is too incredible for acceptance and we are driven to the reasonable conclusion that a Supreme Intelligence is behind all things, manifest in primordial creation, in the life of the universe and in the continual operation of natural laws.

The Realm of Values

A belief in God finds additional justification when we enter the realm of values. The work of the scientist is descriptive, while that of the philosopher or the religionist is interpretative. The chemist or biologist who attempts to explain the natural world in terms of physico-chemical change ignores completely the meaning or worth of anything, yet it is clear that beauty, goodness, love, honor and sacrifice are as truly a part of reality as the chemical union of hydrogen and oxygen in water, or the unfailing law of gravitation. Moral personality must be considered as truly a part of the universal process of development as the biological rise of man. Consider the mother who pours out her strength in tender ministry to her sick child, or the father who takes his hard-earned savings of a lifetime and spends them prodigally on a son's education. The scientist laboring in his laboratory to conquer some insidious disease, the social worker seeking to correct the maladjustments of family life, the missionary giving his life for an alien people, all testify to the presence of values in the sum total of Reality. Who can number the world's heroes who have been concerned with these higher considerations, people like Father Damien working for the lepers in Molokai, Lincoln seeking to free the slaves, or Jane Addams laboring to improve the slums of Chicago. But inanimate creation shows no interest in such struggles, and mere mechanism is indifferent to them. Only Mind is capable of appreciating them and understanding them so that all great virtues, all sublime aspirations speak to us of a God in whose life they are fully realized.

All of these observations lead to faith in God as the most reasonable explanation for our universe. Such a belief is not simply a pious hope. It is a satisfying certainty, a conclusion not blindly reached but resting upon the demands of intelligence. But a conception of God as the reality behind the universal mystery, as First Cause, or as creative Mind Energy, may seem lacking in the personal qualities which we have been accustomed to associate with deity. Is God a being with whom we may have fellowship and social intercourse? This is our next insistent interrogation.

Is God Personal?

The earliest records of the Bible indicate that the Jews were accustomed to think of deity as personal. The Creation story speaks of God walking in the garden in the cool of the day. He talked with Adam and Eve, He covered a cleft in the rock with His hand in order that Moses, who was hidden within, might not look upon God's face and die. It was very natural that the Jewish people, with their simple and devout faith, should think of God in this anthropomorphic manner. This same idea is recognized also in the New Testament, where, in the Book of the Revelation, we find God portrayed as an awe-inspiring figure seated upon a throne in heaven directing the affairs of the universe. Christian art has carried out this thought in portrayals of God as a glorified man, as for example, the remarkable frescoes of Michelangelo on the ceiling of the Sistine Chapel in Rome. In one of the panels God is shown as a benign and patriarchal person with definitely Jewish features, flowing beard, conventional robes, and with all other human attributes.

Any thoughtful person will recognize that we can no longer hold to an anthropomorphic conception of God with a body of human likeness. Such a notion would presume that God had physical organs like our own and that He had sensory experiences of touch, taste, hearing and sight.

Such a thought is too limited in its scope and too crassly materialistic in its conception. Yet this does not mean that we cannot think of God as personal, nor that we must cease to interpret Him in the categories of human experience.

It would be well for us to formulate clearly in our minds what we mean by the term "person," since intellectual confusion often results from vagueness of definition. A person is a self-conscious being capable of rational thought and self-control. This involves the capacity to will, for there could be no self-control without the exercise of the will. It implies also the ability to seek definite ends, for, if there is self-control, a being may move in the direction of his own choosing. Professor Clarence A. Beckwith, in his book *The Idea of God,* holds that this capacity to attain ends is the outstanding characteristic of personality, and he contends that the more personal we are, the more definite is our desire to attain certain ends.

It has already been indicated that the universe suggests rational thought behind it. Modern scientists, like Dr. J. W. Simpson of New College, Edinburgh, recognize that the world process shows a broadly progressive character, and is sus-

tained in a particular direction. It is impossible
to conceive the natural universe with its manifold
evidences of rationality and directive action without postulating self-consciousness and will behind
it. If God does not possess these characteristics,
then man, who is the supreme expression of creative power, is greater than that which produced
him. This directive quality in the universe supports the belief in a Personal God.

However, God is not limited by the personal,
and it would be more accurate to think of Him
as super-personal. Personality is the highest term
we know for the interpretation of human experience, and we are justified in using it to make
clear our idea of God, but God may be more than
personal or less than personal. God may be Force,
as when He is expressed in the flaming thunder-
bolt or in the pull of gravitation. He may be Law
as He is, when revealed in the changing seasons,
the reactions in the chemical laboratory, or the
rhythm of the stellar universe. But there is nothing distinctly personal in a Force or an isolated
law of nature. God may be super-personal in His
potential capacity to create new forms of matter
or energy. Every change in the evolutionary process indicates an element of newness in the world.

Likewise, he may be super-personal in His power to achieve that which the human mind has not yet fathomed.

One of the difficulties into which we fall when we seek the personality of God arises from our thought that Personality must be associated with a physical body or a brain. Human life makes it clear that a person is not a body. If such were the case, our persons would become large when we become stout, and small when we become thin. When a body is mutilated by amputation, the ego, or self, remains intact. The body is simply the instrument through which a person or a soul expresses itself. Nor should personality be confused with the brain. This complex organism is simply an instrument by means of which the physical body performs the bidding of the self. Whole areas of the brain may be atrophied, as Dr. W. Hanna Thomson has pointed out in *Brain and Personality,* and, outside of certain limitations placed upon the physical organism, the self goes on. A person is the manifestation of a Will, and wherever there is evidence of the action of a Will such as we find in the universe there, also, is evidence for personality. The idea of a personal

God can still be held, even though we think of God as the totality of all things and the summation of all values.

May God Be Localized?

We often speak of a person as being in a certain place. But can a person really be localized? Of course, a body may be spatially situated, but this is not necessary for personality. The world is filled with millions of people. We have seen the human machines through which their life is expressed, but we have never seen them. We have seen only the physical vehicle which they use. The best we can say regarding the location of a person is that he is present wherever his personality asserts itself. The speaker on the radio is in every home where he is heard. The person of an author is revealed to every one who reads his book. God is present in every blade of grass, in every mountain stream, in every distant star or planet. He is present in human life and in social relations. God is everywhere, the totality of all his manifestations in the physical and mental realm, and yet He is personal, as definitely and distinctly so as any one of us. The only difference is that the expression of our personalities is restricted, whereas

God's personality is revealed in unlimited forms and in unnumbered ways.

Why Do We Call God Father?

God is called Father because that is the best category of human thought for the interpretation of personality, and consequently it is natural to use that term regarding Him. God could properly be called Mother-God as well as Father-God. In *Science and Health with Key to the Scriptures* Mary Baker Eddy sets forth what she considers the spiritual sense of the Lord's Prayer, and she interprets the first words "Our Father" to mean "Our Father-Mother God." The term "Brother" would likewise express some of the qualities of God, and we often speak of Jesus, in whom God was most perfectly revealed, as our elder Brother. But human society has largely been worked out along patriarchal lines, which makes the use of a thought of God as Father particularly suitable. In addition to ideas of tenderness, love and gentleness suggested by motherhood, there are added in the ideal of Fatherhood such ideas as strength, leadership and protection.

Jesus has established himself as the greatest spiritual Seer that the world has known, and his chief contribution to the conception of God was in his emphasis on the thought of God as Father. The Jews looked upon God as a Creator, a Law-giver, a holy and austere Judge, but Jesus' idea was much loftier. He emphasized the thought of Fatherhood. We follow him, and we choose the highest form for conveying our idea of deity when we refer to God as Father.

May We Define God?

It is impossible for us to define God completely. The best we can do is to observe some of His characteristics. God is first Cause, He is Law, He is Mind, the totality of all things, the summation of all values, the philosophical Absolute. But supremely, God is a Person with qualities of goodness and of love. He knows and cares for man, the supreme product of His handiwork, whom He has created to have fellowship with Him. Nothing which modern science has contributed nor philosophy has brought to light need take from us the assurance of companionship and friendship with Him. The devout worshippers of other generations were limited in their thought about God, and often wrong in their conceptions, but their spiritual sense was right when they con-

ceived the supreme Being as One whom they
could know and trust, whose life and purpose
they could share and whose love encompassed
them always even as the heavens encompass the
earth.

The Pragmatic Test

If one has difficulty with a belief in God it is
well to give that great idea a pragmatic test to see
if it works. Let us inquire whether the integra-
tion of all that is manifested in the idea of God
does not give the most complete and satisfying
explanation of the universe that may be found.
Countless thousands have based their lives on
such an assertion of faith, and it has given them
a dignity of soul, a nobility of spirit, a meaning
and purpose which has uplifted and inspired
them. Burdened by a consciousness of sin, men
have found a sense of pardon through Him. Beaten
and bruised by the vicissitudes of changing for-
tune, He has brought light and hope, and has restored confidence and trust to those lost in the
shadows of despair.

On the shield of the state of Michigan is a Latin
phrase, which when translated means: "If you

seek a beautiful peninsula, look about you." So if one seeks God, let him look around. He is everywhere, beneath our feet, in the mystery of the heavens, in the lives of men, and in the expression of all that is beautiful and good and true.

CHAPTER V

Who Was This Man Jesus?

IF THE Founder of the Christian religion is to be
clearly understood, we must know him as an historical figure, living a life like our own, in a definite period of time, and sharing the limitations
of common humanity. The real Jesus of Nazareth
has been so obscured by the maze of theological
discussions and doctrinal beliefs surrounding his
name, that his human nature has been overshad-
owed and his earthly career surrounded with an
element of unreality. Men have argued about his
preëxistence, his place in the Trinity, his miraculous powers, until they have lost sight of the
gracious and noble Galilean who moved in and
out among his fellow countrymen, dining at their
tables, ministering to their needs and startling
them by words of wisdom such as they had never
heard before.

A few radical scholars have sought to deny the
historicity of Jesus, seeking to identify his origin
with the myth of an ancient sun-god or to consider him simply as the mental projection of an

ideal. Such notions are not worthy of consideration, since they do not harmonize with the documentary evidence or the obvious testimony of history. The Gospel narratives, the letters of St. Paul
and the other writings of the early church witness
to the reality of his earthly life as truly and as
reliably as do the secular writings which verify
other historical personages of the same period.
The existence of the Christian church supports
their words with irrefutable corroboration, and
we may believe that Jesus lived with as much
assurance as we acknowledge Julius Caesar or the
Ptolemies of Egypt.

When Was Jesus Born?

Jesus Christ was not born in the first year of
the present Christian era, as our present method
of reckoning would suggest, but began his life
from six to eight years before that date. This
anomalous fact is easy to explain. It finds its
origin in the mistake of a good priest whose piety
is responsible for the practice we now follow of
dating events "in the year of our Lord." This
man was Dionysius Exiguus, a native of Scythia,
who lived in the sixth century and was one of
the great scholars of his day. Through careful

studies he sought to determine the exact time of Jesus' birth, and he came to the conclusion, after earnest investigation, that the Christian era began seven hundred and fifty-four years after the founding of Rome, which event had heretofore been used as the basis for figuring time. But he made an error of at least six years in his estimates, as was later discovered. The date of Jesus' birth can be fairly well determined through Herod, the Jewish king, who ruled at the time. It will be remembered that "Jesus was born in Judea in the days of Herod the king" (Matthew 2:1). His nativity must have preceded the monarch's death by as much as two years, since Herod's edict to slaughter little children sought to include Jesus by naming children up to that age in the sentence of death. Herod's death is now considered by scholars to have occurred about 750 A. U. C. (*anno urbis conditae*—in the year of the building of the city), and this would place the birth of Jesus not later than 748 or 749 A. U. C., and possibly before that time. Dionysius designated the beginning of the Christian era as 754 A. U. C. and thus made an error of at least six years. His scheme for reckoning time did not become effective until three centuries after his own death, and when computations began under the system *Anno Domini,* the original error had not been discovered.

The exact day of the week and month of the year when Jesus was born are also uncertain, and critical scholars have been unable to agree in their opinions. It was not until the fourth century that the twenty-fifth of December was chosen as the proper date, and tradition has continued to support that day down to the present time. It has been suggested that the date may have been selected to keep members of the early Christian congregations from pagan feasts and celebrations which took place at that season of the year.

Of course, these curious and interesting facts about the life of Jesus do not affect his place in history in the slightest degree. They do make us aware of the lack of detailed records such as are kept in our own time, and which, if available, would make his reality even more vivid for us.

Racial Background

Jesus was a Jew. He lived in the southern part of Syria at the eastern end of the Mediterranean sea, in the country called Palestine. This land had been occupied for thirteen centuries by the peo-

ple of his race, who had made their way out of
bondage in Egypt and had taken possession of this
fertile and promising territory. The little nation
of Jews endured much suffering, because their
country was a buffer one between Rome and
Babylon, Assyria and Egypt. When one of these
mighty states moved against another, the Jews
inevitably suffered. In their efforts, as a smaller
power, to strengthen their own position, they
made alliances, first with one nation and then
another, and not infrequently the results were
disastrous. Out of the bitterness and tragedy of
suffering the Jews were driven to a deep dependence upon their God, Yahweh, and from that
devotion there developed a piety that made them
the most religious nation in the ancient world.

Jesus was born in a simple Jewish home which
had shared the bitter suffering of the nation, and
which reflected the religious spirit which marked
the life of his race. His father, who was named
Joseph, was a carpenter by trade. His mother,
who was called Mary, was a pious, devoted soul,
who exerted a powerful influence on the plastic,
growing mind of her Son. Jesus had four brothers, James, Joseph, Judas, and Simon, and two
or more sisters whose names are not known (Mat-

thew 13:55-56). These were probably half-brothers and sisters through his father, Joseph, by a former marriage.

Early Life

The immediate circumstances of Jesus' birth are interesting. An edict had gone forth from Caesar Augustus for an enrolment of all the people in the Roman empire, much like a census that we would take to-day. The residents of Palestine were expected to report in the towns which were the ancestral homes of their people. As Joseph and Mary were descendants of David, and as Bethlehem was the home of David, they made a trip to that place, five miles south of Jerusalem, in order to carry out this imperial mandate. When they reached their destination, so many others had preceded them, for the same purpose, that the village inn was crowded to capacity and they could secure no accommodations there. Continuing their search for a place to rest, they ultimately found lodging in a cave in the limestone rocks of the region, which was used as a stable for animals. It was a lowly shelter, indeed, and the room reeked with the odor of sweating beasts of burden, but it was a welcome haven, for Mary's time of delivery had come and here she gave birth to her first child. As Giovanni Papini has said with striking phrase: "The filthiest place in the world was the first room of the only pure man ever born of woman." Tradition has it that there were unusual portents in the skies which marked the auspicious event, that shepherds heard angelic voices announcing Jesus' coming, and that wise men from the East laid costly gifts at his feet. All of these accounts are beautifully preserved for us in our Christmas tradition.

Eight days after Jesus' birth, he was circumcised, in accordance with the requirements of the Jewish law, and given his name. He was called Joshua, which means "one who saves." The Greek form of this word is Jesus, and this is the one now universally used in Christendom. Forty days after the nativity, Joseph and Mary went to the Temple at Jerusalem for a two-fold purpose. It had originally been the practice of the Hebrew people to give the first-born son to the service of God: but after the priesthood came definitely under the tribe of Levi, the Jews of other tribes bought back their first born from God by a redemption tax of five shekels. The parents desired to fulfill this conventional requirement. This was

also the time to offer sacrifices for the mother,
who remained ceremonially unclean up to that
time. The customary sacrifice was a lamb and two
doves, but if the family happened to be in modest
circumstances, only the two doves were offered.
When Joseph and Mary had paid the necessary
redemption tax and had completed their sacrificial service, they returned to Nazareth. Tradition has it that Herod, the Jewish king, had heard
a rumor that a new king had been born among
his people, and fearing the loss of his own position, sought to forestall such an eventuality by a
slaughter of little children. To avoid the dire results of such an edict, the godly parents took their
little son into Egypt, where they remained until
Herod's death. On their return to Palestine they
reëstablished their home in Nazareth.

Jesus' parents must have been moderately poor,
and we may imagine the type of home in which
he lived. It was doubtless a one-room house with
simple equipment and few material comforts.
Joseph earned a modest livelihood from his work
as a carpenter, making ox-yokes, wooden plows
and furniture, and also doing general repair
work. Jesus must have been around his father's
shop much as a son might be to-day. Possibly he

helped with some of the simpler tasks. He received the customary education of Jewish children. This would give him an acquaintance with
the Torah, the writings of the Prophets and the
great hymns of Psalms with which the people
comforted themselves. In his public ministry he
gave evidence of wide familiarity with the Scriptures of his people, and that knowledge must
have been acquired when he was still young.
There is no doubt that his noble mother played
an important part in this early training, and, later,
it was to exert an immeasurable influence on his
life.

The Years of Silence

Outside of these early incidents, we have almost no record for the first thirty years of Jesus'
life. We get one fleeting glimpse of him, at the
age of twelve, when his parents took him to
Jerusalem for the feast of the Passover. After the
ceremonies were over and they had started home,
they discovered that Jesus was not in the crowd
with which they were travelling. Hurrying back
to the city, they were amazed to find him in the
Temple carrying on a religious discussion with the
wise men there. His remarks to his parents on

that occasion indicated clearly that already he had developed a sense of deep obligation to God which, in his mind, took precedence even over duty to his parents.

Some have conjectured that the subsequent life of Jesus showed such unique and unusual spiritual insight that during these years of silence he must have travelled far, possibly to India, and there have come under the influence of religious teachers. This is simply an idle conjecture originating in a desire to explain his unusual knowledge and his great spiritual power, and is not substantiated by any trustworthy evidence. The facts would suggest that he remained at home, sharing in the life of his own people but manifesting a rare and unusual interest in all things pertaining to the religious life.

The Public Career of Jesus

At the age of thirty Jesus commenced his public career. He had been much impressed by a rough and influential prophet, called John the Baptist, who was calling the populace to repentance for their sins and to preparation for the coming of the Messiah, for whom the Jews had waited anxiously through the centuries. John's

ascetic manner and his picturesque figure attracted many to him, and his virile message created a profound impression. On the occasion of
Jesus' journey to Jerusalem for the celebration
of the Feast of Tabernacles, he accepted from
John the rite of baptism in the Jordan. This great
preacher used this ceremonial act as a symbol of
the washing away of sin and the purpose of the
believer to live a clean, pure life in accordance
with the will of God. An overwhelming conviction dawned on Jesus at the time of his baptism
that motivated all the rest of his earthly life.
Then it was that he became aware that he was to
be the fulfilment of the dream of the Jewish nation, that he was to be the Messiah who should
lead his people in the ways of righteousness and
truth. After this profound inner experience,
which came to him at the time of his baptism, he
retired into a desert place for communion and
meditation. While there, he was confronted with
great temptations, which are described in the
Scriptures as conversations with the devil. We
may be sure that no flesh and blood being was
actually with him, no physical devil who per-
sonified the spirit of evil in the world. Jesus' experience was a mental one, and was the result

of his overwhelming consciousness of spiritual power. He was able to conquer these impulses to use his gifts for base and ignoble ends, and to see his spiritual destiny in true perspective. After that inner victory, he returned to his home town and his own people to begin his public ministry.

Jesus proclaimed his message first in the synagogue of Nazareth. The people were amazed at his teachings, and were wrathful because of the claims he made for himself. They had known him simply as one of the boys of the village who had grown to manhood in their midst, the son of the carpenter Joseph, and not as one who could be considered a prophet from God. Undismayed by their rebuff, he turned to Capernaum to proclaim the conviction that was burning in his own soul. One of his first public acts was to call four fishermen into his service. These were Simon and his brother Andrew, James and his brother John. Later, eight others were selected and became his close disciples. In his public discourses Jesus attracted much attention by his own winsome personality. The faith which he engendered resulted in the healing of a number of cases of illness. Some of his teaching was in public, while at other times he spoke privately to intimate groups. On one memorable trip to Jerusalem he attracted much attention by purging the Temple of those who were using it for commercial and dishonorable purposes. During his first year of public ministry, which was probably spent largely in Judea, he came gradually to the attention of the people. Later he travelled in Galilee, where he met with a large measure of public favor. His teachings regarding the Kingdom of God and his healing ministry were such as to make him popular among an eager and suffering nation.

For nearly three years Jesus continued his preaching, until his opponents became convinced that he was a menace to the established tradition and to the life of the Jewish religion. So they determined to destroy him. When the chosen time had come, one of his disciples, Judas by name, turned traitor and betrayed him into the hands of his adversaries. While he was in the garden of Gethsemane, to which place he had retreated with his disciples for the purpose of prayer, they seized him and took him to the home of Annas, the father-in-law of the high priest. On the following morning he was tried before the Sanhedrin. In the presence of that august body of religious leaders he was accused of blasphemy. False witnesses appeared against him and when, in answer to a question, he acknowledged publicly that he was Christ, they demanded that he be put to death. Knowing that the Law did not permit them to execute this sentence themselves, they turned to Pontius Pilate, the Roman ruler of Judea, for the accomplishment of their nefarious purpose. Pilate examined him but could find no cause for such drastic action. He was disposed to let Jesus go, but being unwilling to face possible trouble from an enraged and excited populace he consented that a sentence of death should be executed. By this single act of compromise with his own best judgment Pilate has become the world's symbol of weakness and moral ineptitude. Punishment by death meant crucifixion. That ignominious method of destroying human life was common in ancient times. Josephus, the Jewish historian, informs us that scourging always preceded crucifixion, and the unfortunate victim had to submit not only to that indignity, but also endure the raillery and the rough play of the soldiers. These cruel injustices were heaped upon Jesus, and after the bestial impulses of his detractors had been given full expression, he was led away to his death. Jesus was taken outside the walls of Jerusalem for the execution of the sentence. The hill on which his cross was placed was called Golgotha, because of its resemblance to a skull. There he was hung between two common criminals—the victim of the bitterness and the wrath of the narrow and bigoted religious leaders of his time. He lingered upon the cross from nine o'clock in the morning until three o'clock in the afternoon, when a merciful death brought an end to his physical suffering and his pure soul found its way back to God. On the third day after this important event, the discouraged and disheartened disciples became convinced that he was alive, and that glorious assurance of his resurrection and his triumph over the forces of evil has been the sublime faith of Christian believers until the present time.

Such is the narrative, in brief and fragmentary form, of the earthly life of Jesus. What caused his untimely end? Undoubtedly it was an over-zealous nationalism and the fear that the traditional faith of Judaism might be destroyed by his message.

The Message of Jesus

Two great conceptions were prominent in
Jesus' message—the Fatherhood of God, and the
brotherhood of man. The Jews had stressed the
holiness of God, His justice, His power and His
omnipotence, but Jesus made it clear that God
could best be understood through an interpretation of Him as Father. He illustrated this great
belief by three noble parables of the lost boy, the
lost sheep, and the lost coin. A logical corollary
of this primal idea was his insistence that all men
are brothers. This sublime Truth permeates all
his teachings like the sunshine of a summer's day.
He not only taught brotherhood, but he demonstrated his belief in many ways, such as dining
with publicans and sinners, helping the Syro-
Phoenician woman who did not belong to the
house of Israel, and gently ministering to the sick
and afflicted.

His teachings differed from the commonly accepted notions of the synagogue in his insistence
upon a spiritual interpretation of the Law and
the Prophets, rather than the legal and traditional
one. His attitude toward the Sabbath furnishes a
striking illustration. Moses had said, "Remember

the Sabbath day to keep it holy." Around that important religious injunction the rabbis had developed innumerable restrictions. A man could not carry a loaf of bread upon the Sabbath day. If a wine cask sprang a leak, a piece of wax could not be pushed into the crack on that holy day. If a hand was injured the wound could not be washed upon the Sabbath unless there was danger that serious results might ensue. If a man rinsed his mouth with vinegar, and the vinegar was spewed out on the ground, he was guilty of working on the day of rest, but if he swallowed the vinegar, it was considered food, and eating was permissible. To such legally-bound people Jesus said, "The Sabbath was made for man and not man for the Sabbath."

There are frequent references in Jesus' teachings to the Kingdom of God. This idea is associated with the hope, which continually asserted itself in the minds of the Jewish people, that some day their nation would be restored to a position of preëminence and power such as it enjoyed in the days of the great king David. The circumstances of the years tended to work against the establishment of a great and influential nation, but the hope continued to persist. It was believed that some day a ruler would come who would be the Messiah, an anointed one from God, who would be of the seed of David and who would bring material prosperity and national strength to God's people. The Messianic hope was prominent in the thought of the people when Jesus was alive. Side by side with that great anticipation was another idea, which is associated with the term "Son of Man." Since there was no outward evidence of return of material power through the ordinary channels of victory on the field of battle and success against powerful kingdoms, there developed the feeling that in His own time God would send a Supernatural Being who would realize His purpose by a mighty and catastrophic stroke, in which the Jews would be restored to power. It is evident that Jesus was clearly familiar with these two great hopes of his own people, and that he felt his own life was to be the fulfilment both of the Jewish longing for a Messiah and their hope for the coming of the Son of Man. He used both of these terms with reference to himself, but gave them an interpretation quite different from the materialistic notions of his day.

He thought of a spiritual kingdom which would
be set up in human hearts and which would represent the coming of God's reign in a true and
living sense, a kingdom dominated by the power
of spiritual truth and so able to conquer all adversaries. In his combination of these two ideas in
this unusual and spiritualized way, Jesus revealed
an originality and an insight that betokened the
greatness of his teaching and made him stand out
as a true prophet and ambassador of God.

His teaching regarding the Messianic hope of
Judaism was particularly offensive to his opponents. The Pharisees felt that his origin was too
humble for such a claim, that his followers came
from the lower ranks of society and that he himself did not show the proper allegiance to the
rituals and practices of the Jewish people. All of
these conditions contradicted the popular ideas
of the day regarding the expected Messiah.

The message of Jesus is marked by frequent
use of parables. This method was in common use
in his time and was very effective, for the human
mind has ever been able to grasp concrete ideas
more easily than abstract ones. There are thirty-
eight of these parabolic utterances in the teach-

ings of Jesus. Some of them are as beautiful in form and expression as anything which can be found anywhere in the whole realm of literature. His two greatest parabolic discourses are the parables of the prodigal son and the good Samaritan. In the first, Jesus portrays his major idea of Fatherhood, and reveals the illimitable love of God, which never wavers, despite human weaknesses and shortcomings, but goes out perpetually to man until the wanderer is back in the Father's home. The second parable stresses Jesus' ideal of brotherhood, with its insistence on good will for all classes and conditions of men. It should be said here, by way of interpolation, that if we are going to interpret these or other parables of Jesus correctly, we must not attempt to carry the analogy to every detail of the stories but to grasp the fundamental Truth hidden in each one of them as the main purpose for which the narrative was told.

It has been claimed by some that Jesus brought nothing original in his message, and that all of his ideas may be found in the writings of the Old Testament or in the teachings of the great religious leaders of his day. It must be admitted that Jesus emphasized much that had been said before. His statement regarding the greatest commandments of the Law furnishes a striking example. But he must be given credit for sifting essentials from non-essentials and for the way in which he vivified and vitalized old religious Truth. What is more, his emphasis on certain ideas which he considered especially important, and his interpretation of the Kingdom of God as a spiritual reality, were tantamount to the presentation of entirely new religious ideas.

The person of Jesus represents such a perfect union of lofty spiritual idealism and faultless moral conduct that he stands absolutely unique in the annals of human history. No one has ever been found who has even approximated the perfection which his life has revealed, and it has been the dispassionate judgment of history that he has given the world a standard which, if honestly followed, will bring not only abundant life to the individual, but good will and brotherhood to all people.

In one of his poems, Sidney Lanier reviews the great religious leaders of history, and then turning to Christ, says:

"But thee, but thee, O Sovereign Seer of time,
    But thee, O man's best Man, O love's best
       Love,
O perfect Life in perfect labor writ,
    O, all men's Comrade, Servant, Priest or King,
"O, what amiss may I forgive in Thee,
    Jesus, good Paragon, thou crystal Christ."

Such is the witness of all who have sought to follow the historic Jesus, and who have claimed him as their own.

CHAPTER VI

Did Jesus Rise from the Dead?

THERE are two observations which very properly may be made at the beginning of any consideration of the resurrection of Jesus. While they are quite obvious, they should both be recognized. First, the resurrection of a dead person to life is contrary to customary human experience. Medical science records isolated cases in which respiration has stopped and the heart has ceased to beat, and yet by means of artificial respiration or by the use of powerful drugs, the regular functions of the body have been resumed. But in these instances the lapse of time has been negligible, for only a few moments at the most, and it may be seriously questioned whether death occurred at all. If Jesus actually rose from the dead, as is claimed for him, it is a unique fact in human history with no parallel in the observations and records of men. The very unusual character of this claim is such as to cause scientifically-trained persons to doubt its authenticity or categorically to deny it altogether. Of course, the truly scientific mind does not assert that anything is impossible, but a reported phenomenon of an isolated character raises doubts regarding its authenticity.

The second fact is an historical one which deserves as much consideration as the first. It may be stated simply. The Christian church has accepted and believed in the resurrection of Jesus throughout all its history despite the rareness of the occurrence and the intellectual doubts which have been raised about it. A faith that Jesus rose from the dead was an outstanding characteristic of the apostolic church and has been the sublime conviction of Christian believers for nearly twenty centuries. The greatest festal day in the church year is Easter, at which time devout worshippers the world over acknowledge a risen Christ and pledge renewed allegiance to him.

Therefore, it becomes our duty, in seeking an answer to the question: "Did Jesus rise from the dead?" to consider these antithetical realities with the greatest care and to seek to do justice to both of them. After examining the evidence, we must determine whether the facts are sufficiently convincing to justify a belief in the resurrection, or whether absolute honesty demands that we repudiate it. Since this event is remotely dated in history and is not within the scope of our own personal experience, we must rely on documentary evidence, and faith will be conditioned by the credence we give to the writings in which the resurrection is recorded. The Bible is our chief source of information.

Evidence for the Resurrection

Regardless of the value we may place on the moral teaching of the books of the New Testament, we must admit that they are well authenticated documents, worthy of as much consideration as any ancient writings. No literature has been given more careful scrutiny or more painstaking examination. Since the books were written by different authors at different times, each one may be considered separately, and the testimony of many writers should receive greater weight than the witness of a single person.

The gospel narratives and the writings of Paul testify to nine different instances in which Jesus appeared after his crucifixion. They are as follows:-

1. Mary Magdalene and the other Mary—Matthew 28:9.
2. Mary Magdalene—Mark 16:9, John 20:14.
3. Cephas—Luke 24:34; I Corinthians 15:5.
4. To two Disciples—Mark 16:12, Luke 24:15.
5. To the Disciples—Matthew 28:17, Mark 16:14, Luke 24:36, John 20:19, I Corinthians 15:5.
6. To the Disciples a second time—John 20:26.
7. To the Disciples at Tiberius—John 21:1ff.
8. To five hundred at once—I Corinthians 15:6.
9. To James—I Corinthians 15:7, also Gospel to the Hebrews (Apocryphal).

The earliest writings of the New Testament come from Paul, and his closeness to the times of Jesus and his intimate connection with the early church make his testimony very valuable. Paul was absolutely certain that Jesus rose from the dead. His statement to the church at 'Corinth makes his position very clear. "For I delivered unto you first of all that which also I received: that Christ died for our sins according to the Scriptures; and that he was buried; and that he hath been raised on the third day according to the Scriptures; and that he appeared to Cephas; then to the twelve; then he appeared to above five hundred brethren at once, of whom the greater part remain until now, but some are fallen asleep; then he appeared to James; then to all the apostles; and last of all, as to the child untimely born, he appeared to me also" (I Corinthians 15:3-9). All of Paul's teaching rests on a firm belief that Jesus conquered death, and it was a central idea in his whole theological system. He could not have spoken with such boldness on this point unless his conviction were based on sources which he considered absolutely truthworthy.

Each one of the biographers or narrators of the life of Jesus shared this same thought. Their honesty is unimpeachable, and they were so certain that Jesus made himself known after the crucifixion that they laid great stress upon that fact in their writings. It is significant that all four of them record the appearance of Jesus to his disciples, and each individually reports other instances as well. There are some variations in details, but they are not more than one would expect from different persons dealing with events in their own particular manner and relying on oral rather than written tradition. While Matthew and Luke had Mark as one of their sources of information, neither would have included the resurrection in his gospel narrative if he had doubted the accuracy of the fact. Luke, in the Acts of the Apostles, attributes a particularly noteworthy passage to Peter, one of the original disciples. He is recorded as saying of Jesus on the Day of Pentecost: "Him, being delivered up by the determinate counsel and foreknowledge of God, ye, by the hands of lawless men did crucify and slay, whom God raised up, having loosed the pangs of death, because it was not possible that He should be holden of it" (Acts 2:23 ff).

The close proximity of Paul and the Evangelists to the times of Jesus, and their reports of many post-resurrection appearances, establish a strong presumption that we are dealing with fact and not with fancy. The large number of persons reported to have seen a risen Christ adds weight to the evidence. If Jesus did not rise from the dead, then these writers may be accused of circulating a false story about him among people who must have known Jesus personally or who were acquainted with his disciples. They would have had plenty of opportunity to be advised of their error and to have had suspicion cast upon their faith. But that faith persisted, and they passed on their conviction to posterity in plain, clear, unequivocal language incapable of misunderstanding.

What Happened to the Disciples?

After Jesus was crucified, the disciples were a discouraged, downhearted group. They had little faith that they would see their Friend again. Even when they were told that Jesus had risen from the dead they were unwilling to believe. The One in whom they had trusted had been destroyed, they themselves were fortunate not to have suffered a similar fate, and their hopes and dreams had been cast into the dust. Then something happened, and overnight they were changed from a mood of deep despair into a group of enthusiastic, confident men who were certain that Jesus was alive. That burning ecstasy in their hearts was not extinguished until death had overtaken them. They preached a message of a risen Christ, One who had come back to them and demonstrated that he was Lord of life and Conqueror of death. There is no reasonable explanation for this changed spirit in the disciples if the resurrection did not occur.

That same faith of the disciples was the faith of the early church. It appeared in the first decades of the church's life, and has perpetuated itself to the present time as one of the sure and certain convictions of those who call themselves Christian. The church was reared upon the rock of the resurrection. How could such a conviction have become so firmly rooted unless founded upon a fact which the first century Christians considered reliable?

The Establishment of the First Day of the Week

Another significant fact is the establishment of the first day of the week as a day of rest and worship. The early Christians were Jews, steeped in the tradition of their forefathers, and they had a deep and sacred veneration for the seventh day as the day holy to the Lord. Had not he commanded them to "remember the Sabbath day to keep it holy"? Yet very soon we find these devout Jews substituting for that day another one which they felt to be even more sacred than the Sabbath. The day they came to revere was the first day of the week, being that on which Jesus rose from the dead. The day of Pentecost was also on the first day of the week, and that event must have added importance and significance to the celebration of Sunday, yet its influence is not to be compared with that of the resurrection in bringing about this radical change in the firmly established customs of the people.

We conclude, therefore, that the testimony of the documents, the change of the disciples' attitude and the establishment of Sunday as the day of rest furnish incontrovertible evidence for an unusual fact, and one which must not be denied simply because we find no parallel for it.

Some Interesting Speculations

Some interesting speculations about the resurrection are worthy of consideration. The occurrence was so rare that other explanations have been sought for the development of this belief. The idea has been advanced that Jesus did not really die upon the Cross but merely swooned. In this condition, he might have appeared dead and have been taken down and placed in a tomb. But there the cool air and the odor of the spices revived him, and he was able to appear afterwards as a living person among his friends. This explanation is ingenious, but does violence to the details of the record. Certainly, his cruel punishment was the kind that ordinarily would have caused death. The tomb in which he was placed was sealed. His resurrection appearances, in some instances at least, indicated that he had a body different from his physical one and, after the disciples and others had seen him, he vanished from their midst. This fantastic theory creates more problems than it explains away, and does too much violence to the testimony to be given credence.

It has also been suggested that Jesus did not really appear after his death but that his disciples were so overwrought, and in such a high state of mental excitement, that they only thought they saw him. In other words, they suffered an hallucination. If Jesus had appeared to only one person who reported afterwards that he had seen him, there would be considerable plausibility to this interpretation. But he appeared not to one person but to many; he appeared not on one occasion but on several. It would require a stretch of the imagination quite beyond the bounds of reason to conclude that all who purported to have seen him were deceived by a figment of the mind. It will also be recalled that the disciples were not in a mood of expectancy concerning the resurrection, and it is hard to understand how their excited emotions would create that which was contrary to their own beliefs.

Still another idea which has also been put forth is that Jesus actually died, but his disciples or friends made their way to his tomb, carried the body away and circulated the report among his followers that he had risen from the dead. This would make faith in the resurrection rest upon pure fraud and deception. But deception is not easy to hide, particularly if several persons are involved. One way that modern crime is discovered is through the disposition of people to talk. A group of lawless men commit an offense against society and then one of them, in an unguarded moment, reveals a secret which brings the offense of all to the light. To accept this notion would require a faith in a conspiracy of silence quite contrary to human experience. Each one of the post-resurrection appearances would have to be established on a similar basis of deceit, and such a theory, in the light of the attested facts, becomes altogether unreasonable.

Is There a Scientific Explanation for the Resurrection?

Absolute honesty demands that we admit that there is no scientific explanation for the resurrection which can be given in terms of our present knowledge. No one knows how a dead person could become alive after the life processes have ended. But it is quite unscientific to cast aside any real fact simply because we cannot explain it. Life is filled with mystery, and there are many realities which baffle our powers to comprehend but which must be acknowledged as true despite our ignorance. No one can explain life itself. The amoeba, a simple unicellular animal with central nucleus and surrounding protoplasm, has the ability to move, to assimilate food, to elongate and produce another amoeba, and in these elemental capacities of its microscopic existence it holds a secret that all the wisdom of scientists has been unable to explain. The fact is there, but the explanation is still as far away as the dawn of created life. The pull of gravitation is apparent in all the natural universe. Every child who tosses a ball into the air has a concrete demonstration of it. The trees that grow straight upward on a sloping hillside are silent witnesses to its continued operation. But who can tell what gives this peculiar property to matter, present in the tiniest grain of sand and operating throughout the whole solar system? If the resurrection is a fact, it must be acknowledged as such whether we can explain it or not, just as we admit the reality of life and of gravitation. A belief in the resurrection is not defended on the basis of any scientific explanation. It rests upon the strong foundation of factual evidence for its reality.

It is not inconceivable that certain individuals might have the capacity to project their personalities from the unseen world into the world of sense, and be able to be recognized by other persons attuned to them by spirit and temperament. The members of the societies for psychical research contend that there are individuals in the physical world, and also in the spiritual world, who possess unusual abilities in this very field in much the same way that others show special talents as artists, musicians, and poets. These are called mediums, or the controls by whom messages are thought to come. It is common testimony that bereaved persons sometimes feel a sense of awareness of the presence of the one whom they have lost, and this feeling in some instances reaches a state of certainty in their minds. Skeptics may dismiss such experiences as purely mental creations brought about through deep emotional strain with no corresponding reality to them. Possibly they are right, but there is also the possibility that the barrier between this life and that beyond the grave is not as great as is sometimes imagined. The complexity of the laws of the physical universe suggest a similar ramification in the psychical realm, and certainly modern studies of the subconscious mind, hypnosis, suggestion and the like, make it clear that the mental life of man is still a vast unexplored, undiscovered country. The personality of Jesus was so unusual, so compelling, so deeply spiritual, that it would not be strange if some unusual phenomena were associated with him. The powerful radio station is picked up much more easily than a weaker one; so Jesus may have been more able than others to bring an awareness of himself to the disciples whom he had left behind. All of these ideas are purely conjectural, and do not have the seal of scientific approval, but they may indicate something which we are apt to forget, namely, that there are realms of reality not yet entered which some day may be opened to us.

What Kind of a Body Did Jesus Have after the Resurrection?

There are three conclusions which have been reached regarding the body of Jesus after the resurrection. Many of the early Christian Fathers believed that Jesus rose from the dead with the same physical body that he had when he died. Their position is supported by the statements about the empty tomb, by the command given to Thomas to thrust his hand into the wound in Jesus' side (John 2:26), and by the incident where Jesus ate with his disciples (John 21:10ff). Others have held that Jesus had a spiritualized body, which was real, but which did not possess the same characteristics as a physical one. This point of view finds some substantiation in Jesus' admonition to Mary not to touch him (John 20:17), and in the sudden appearance of Jesus in the midst of his disciples when they were in a closed room together (John 20:19ff). The third position was the one held by the Gnostics, one of the sects among the early Christians, who did not believe in any bodily resurrection, but held that the experience was a purely spiritual one.

It has been maintained that the empty tomb furnishes irrefutable proof in favor of the first idea, namely, that Jesus rose with the same body that was crucified on the Cross. But there may be some very natural explanations for the absence of the body in the tomb, as Canon B. H. Streeter has suggested. It may have been removed by Roman soldiers who feared possible disturbances among the Jews. There is also the possibility that the story of the empty tomb, although not established in fact, was an elaboration of the original belief in the resurrection. Under ordinary circumstances we would not lean toward a supernatural interpretation of an event when the possibility of a natural one is present, and particularly in this case when some of the post-resurrection appearances indicate a spiritual body of an entirely different character than a physical one. It is the writer's conviction that Jesus rose with a spiritual body possessing essentially different characteristics than his physical organism. This position seems more consonant with the facts and more appropriate than the traditional belief of a flesh and blood resurrection. It is not likely that in the future life humanity will be clothed with the physical bodies that we have on earth, nor does it seem probable that Jesus had such a body when he made his unusual appearances. However, the important fact to be remembered is that all questions regarding the nature of Jesus' body are secondary to the reality of the resurrection itself.

The resurrection of Jesus was a justification of his own claim that he was the son of God. It was concrete demonstration that spiritual forces cannot be ultimately conquered by material ones. It convinced his followers that their Leader was permanently victorious and greater than all the hosts of evil.

Conclusions

The resurrection of Jesus may be accepted as an historical fact so well authenticated as to permit no denial. To claim that he did not rise from the dead raises more intellectual difficulties than it removes. It calls for some other kind of explanation for the origin of clearly attested documentary evidence, and requires impossible explanations for definite facts in the life and history of the Christian church. While we have no present scientific explanation of this stupendous event of human history, we realize that a greater knowledge of the laws of the mental and spiritual kingdom may some day open the portals of understanding. The problems of the empty tomb and the nature of the resurrection body are incapable of present solution, but they do not destroy the validity of the resurrection itself. The followers of Jesus will continue to believe that the first glorious Easter day vindicated their Master and furnished irrefutable testimony that "Life is ever Lord of death and love can never lose its own."

CHAPTER VII

Was Jesus Divine?

THE divinity of Jesus has been a topic for discussion throughout the entire history of the Christian church. The rudiments of this belief appeared in the first century, and the doctrine has persisted with tenacity through all the succeeding years. Some have accepted it without question; others have denied it vigorously. The subject was a point of controversy between the church and the Ebionites, an early sect of the Jewish Christians, who espoused Gnosticism. It furnished the basis for the disputes at the Council of Nicea in 325 A. D. The Reformers had no unanimity of opinion regarding it, and in modern times the tenet has been a line of cleavage between Trinitarians and Unitarians. The supporters of Jesus' divinity have stoutly maintained that if this fact were denied, Jesus would lose much of his influence and spiritual power. Those who have emphasized his humanity have been equally insistent that any identification of Christ with God removes him from the category of human individuals and so destroys the value of his life for men. Therefore, it becomes important for the modern man who is seeking the Truth to have an intelligent understanding of what is meant when it is said that Jesus is divine.

Jesus a Unique Personality

There is a general consensus of opinion that Jesus was a unique personality in human history. Although all available facts about him have been collated, and his spoken words given searching analysis, he still transcends all powers of description. His life is more than all that may be said about him, and he eludes the most gifted biographers and interpreters. The world has produced many religious seers, but none even approaches him in his far-reaching influence on the world. Outwardly, he lived the life of a Galilean peasant, engaging in normal human activity and sharing all the common experiences of men. Inwardly, he was possessed of a spirit that seems to outreach the bounds of common humanity, standing as One in whom the character and purpose of the eternal God is revealed. It is this amazing quality of the soul, with its subtle mystery, that baffles description and creates a sense of inadequacy in every effort to explain him.

The uncommon nature of Jesus' personality is not something acknowledged only in later centuries, for it was recognized even by his contemporaries. Some looked upon him as a prophet, one of those great messengers of God who appeared from time to time in Jewish history and stirred the hearts of the people. Others considered him a wonder worker whose clear eye, confident manner, and assuring word brought restoring powers of healing. His intimate disciples looked upon him as the fulfillment of the age-long Messianic hope of the Jewish people, and when Peter was asked to express his opinion he exclaimed impulsively: "Thou art the Christ, the son of the living God." The unfolding years have simply added to the veneration in which he was held while living on the earth, so that he emerges from twenty centuries of history as the wonder of all ages, the most baffling and amazing phenomenon in the realm of human personality.

The unfolding of the idea that Jesus was divine is closely related to the influence which he had upon the lives of his followers. They felt that when they were in contact with him they were not

only dealing with some one like themselves, but
some one who was the living expression of God's
own spirit. His life uplifted them; his teachings
inspired them; he made them feel the reality of
the spiritual kingdom. In this sense, the reactions
of the early Christians to Jesus were exactly like
those of his followers to-day. With such influences
playing upon them, it is easy to comprehend how
they began to ascribe divinity to him, and this inclination was the first step in the subsequent tendency to raise him to the level of God Himself. But,
as has often been the case when men have sought
to give a theological interpretation to a valid religious experience, there was a drift away from the
experience itself, and the church became involved
in a labyrinth of philosophical speculations.

An Important Influence

In order to understand this development, we
should know something about a popular Greek
idea of Jesus' day, commonly called the Logos
theory. The Greek philosophers, following the
thought of Plato and the Stoics, held the conception that God was a Being without qualities and
attributes, but that there were a series of emanations called Ideas or Forms which went forth from

Him. The first emanation from God was the Logos, or "the principle of Reason." "Logos" means "word" but as language was peculiar to man, and as speech implies thought, the Logos represents the faculty of reason. This Logos was given characteristics of personality, and was the creator of the world. This point is particularly worthy of observation because of its subsequent relation to Christian thought; namely, that God Himself did not bring the cosmos into form, but this second Being who proceeded from Him. The Gnostics, a group of religious thinkers who selected their ideas from many sources, followed Greek thought in their insistence that God was too pure and refined a Being to bring into existence a world in which evil was present. It was their contention that after many emanations a being known as the Demiurge created the universe. The Demiurge was far enough removed from God Himself, and of sufficiently low degree, to make a world like ours with perfect propriety. These Gnostics insisted that the God of the Jews was not the real God but was only the Demiurge. In a world filled with such complex philosophical speculations Christian thought began to develop. The early Christian writers who were anxious to interpret

Jesus to the Hellenic and Hebraic mind felt that they could make his life more understandable by identifying him with the Logos conception. Justin Martyr was the earliest of the Christian scholars to present such a position, and many others followed him. In the first chapter of the gospel according to St. John the author shows the influence of this trend in the very familiar words: "In the beginning was the Word (Logos), and the Word was with God and the Word was God. The same was in the beginning with God. All things were made through Him and without Him was not anything made that was made."

When Christian thought began to take this direction, it naturally attracted much attention, but it also became very confusing. For example, there was animated discussion whether the emanation of the Logos took anything away from the Being of God so that God was lessened thereby. It was maintained that just as a flame lighted from another blaze takes nothing from its source, so the Logos took nothing from God. Others inquired whether there was ever a time when the Logos did not exist. If so, there must have been a time when Jesus, the incarnation of the Logos, did not exist. This theoretical speculation, which to our minds seems so far removed from practical realities, furnished the basis for one of the bitterest controversies in the long history of the Christian church. The Council of Nicea was assembled in 325 A. D. to settle the matter. Athanasius and his followers asserted that Jesus had existed eternally, while the opposing group led by Arius, a presbyter in Alexandria, maintained that while Jesus was like God he was not identical with God, and there was a time when he did not exist. In this acrimonious dispute Athanasius carried the day, and Arius and his followers were sent into banishment.

Other Difficulties

Another difficulty arose in the efforts to explain how God and man could be united in one person. The church did not wish to deny either the unity of God or the humanity of Jesus. Appolinaris, bishop of Laodicea from 362 to 383 A. D., held that it was impossible for Jesus to have two natures, a human and a divine one, and so, while admitting that Jesus had a human body, he claimed that the Logos took the place of the human soul in Jesus. Nestorius, patriarch of Constantinople, was not satisfied with such an interpretation, despite its ingenuity, and he advanced the contention that the personality of Jesus was a commingling of the human and divine in a single person. He raised another issue in these cumbersome speculations by opposing the idea that Mary, who had given birth to Jesus, was the mother of God. He insisted that Mary was the mother of the human Jesus, but not the mother of the divine Jesus and therefore Mary was not the mother of God. Another great ecclesiastical council was the outgrowth of these logomachies, the Council of Chalcedon, which met in 451 A. D. After much discussion, that assemblage solemnly affirmed: "We recognize one Christ, Son, Lord and only begotten, in two natures, unmingled, immutable, indivisible, inseparable, the difference of the natures being by no means obliterated by the union, but on the contrary, the peculiar nature of each nature being preserved and entering into one person and one hypostasis, not divided nor separated into two persons." A modern man has difficulty in getting anything out of such a pronouncement, but it was quite satisfactory to those who prepared it.

It is not necessary to trace the development in further detail. The remnants of these theological disputations persist even to-day. The Roman

Catholic church preserves the traditional faith in insistence on absolute identity with God, and some of the doctrinal statements of Protestantism hold the same fundamental position. Quite outside of the difficulties in understanding such abstruse statements, the older theologians were evidently much more concerned with problems related to the substance of Jesus than with moral questions associated with his divinity. In the face of these troublesome disputes, we are justified in returning directly to Jesus himself to discover how we can best explain his life. While we should not ignore the earnest and consecrated thought of the great scholars of the church, we are entitled to our own interpretation of Christ in the light of our fullest experience.

What Is Meant by Divinity?

There are two words which have been used in the discussions about Jesus that have been a source of confusion; namely, "deity" and "divinity." Deity involves absolute identity with God, while divinity is not so broad a term and means to "partake of the quality or character of God." If we ascribe deity to Jesus we acknowledge that Jesus was exactly like God in every particular. He would not only have to be the Ultimate Consciousness back of the universe, the Creator of all things, the summation of all values, the philosophical Absolute, but also would have to be omniscient, omnipotent and omnipresent. It is a reasonable step, in determining whether we should hold such a conclusion, to go back to Jesus' life as it has been reported to us. Now, Jesus gave evidence that there were certain limitations to his own personality. He acknowledged openly that there were some things that he did not know—for example, the day and the hour when the Son of Man should come. He felt it necessary to pray for his Father's assistance as he did in the garden of Gethsemane. This fact, if we are to conceive him actually as God, creates a contradiction in itself, for we cannot think of God praying to God. He revealed the common experiences of men, such as surprise, suffering, disappointment, weariness and pain. Certainly absolute candor demands that so far as Jesus' earthly life is set forth in the Bible, he possessed all the limitations of common humanity. We may be eternally grateful for this reality, for it makes it possible for him to be helpful to us in a way that would have been quite impossible if he were a totally different being. It may be argued that although he had a human nature, all the characteristics of God were hidden within his life in some mysterious way which transcends the power of explanation. But he made no claim to such an obscure relation, and from the evidence of the Gospels it may be concluded that such an idea is a man-made theory, produced by abstract theological speculation in order to explain the uniqueness of Jesus' life, and finds no basis in actual facts.

But if "deity" is not the appropriate word to describe Jesus, we may very properly insist that he was divine. In so doing, we are asserting that he possessed "the quality and character of God." Such a fact is inescapable for the vast majority of those who study Jesus' life, but the idea should be carefully examined in order to know its full implication.

Jesus possessed two characteristics that belong to all human beings. He had a body and a soul. But questions of divinity are not related to flesh, blood and bone. Everything that God has created is divine, trees and flowers, beasts of the field, and the body of man himself. But no one would think that Jesus was divine only in the sense that a gigantic oak or a lamb is divine. The real essence of his divinity must be found in his ego, or personality, or soul. We are like God or unlike God in the choices we make, in our moral attitudes, and in the kind of life we live from day to day. The decisions of the will give the soul its moral character. So it was with Jesus.

Wherein Was Jesus Divine?

When we affirm that Jesus was divine, it implies that we have not only a knowledge of the nature of God, but also an understanding of the personality of Jesus, for only as we know God can we compare Jesus to Him, and only as we are familiar with Jesus can we recognize the God-like qualities within him. Thus, this belief must be rooted deeply in human experience. What have we found out about God? One conclusion which we have reached is that He is a self-conscious and a rational Being, guided by a definite will and purpose. We cannot think of God without these attributes, for if He were lacking in them He would be less than man, whose life is ennobled by consciousness and freedom of choice. Likewise, we are certain that ours is a moral universe, and that God is perfectly good. And what do we know about Jesus? He, too, is a self-conscious, rational Being with powers of choice but with all the habiliments of common humanity. Since no question is raised concerning the body of Jesus which is a product of the handiwork of God, and therefore essentially divine, we should look to his inner life and to his moral character for the real depiction of the divine within him.

The moral character of Jesus amazes us by its freedom from an awareness of sin. Not only do we have no record of moral aberration in him, but the Gospels disclose a spiritual leader in whose life there appears not even a cognizance of personal guilt. Great seers like St. Paul, St. Francis and St. Augustine were consumed with a sense of their own shortcomings, and such is invariably the case with sensitive souls. But the intimate conversations of Jesus with his disciples, even in the face of impending death, reveal his conviction that by the purity of his own life men would find deliverance from their sins. Surely Jesus had the power to sin, and the battle which his soul had to wage against temptation is strikingly dramatized in his temptations in the wilderness before his public ministry. Here is an astonishing truth which grips us more firmly in continued studies of Jesus, that an historical person lived with the possibilities of wrong-doing ever before him, and yet with every moral judgment good. It is not strange that Leopold Von Ranke, one of the most eminent historians of the nineteenth century, in his treatise on *The Popes of Rome*, could say of him: "More guiltless and more powerful, more exalted and more holy, has naught ever been on earth than His conduct, His life, and His death; the human race knows nothing that can be brought even afar off into comparison with it."

Our research likewise reveals in Jesus a person completely dominated by a determination to do the highest and the best that he knew. He conceived that highest and best to be the will of God. At no time in his life do we find him yielding to personal comfort or to base and ignoble desires. In private and in public life, he aimed to attain this high goal. For this reason, he proclaimed his message to the world although he knew it would arouse the hostility of the religious leaders of Judaism. For this purpose "He steadfastly set His face toward Jerusalem," though he knew he would meet trouble there. He endured the contumely and the hatred of men, the agonies of the Garden of Gethsemane and the tragedy of Golgotha rather than be false to his ideal. The mind of Jesus was expressed exactly in the words: "My meat is to do the will of His that sent me, and to accomplish His work."

The inner life of Jesus manifests also the motivation of a great love. Love is the noblest quality of the human soul. Nothing so fittingly describes the character of God as this great virtue. God could not be God for men if this were not His attitude. The life of Jesus is the epitome and embodiment of unselfish love. It showed itself in his dealings with little children, in his sympathy for the weak and the oppressed, in his purpose to help even those who would destroy him, and supremely in his prayer upon the Cross for his traducers: "Father forgive them, for they know not what they do!" According to his summation of the Jewish Law, love to God and love to man is the essence of true religion.

Examining the life of Jesus, with its freedom from sin, its complete devotion to the will of God, and its perfect fulfilment of the spirit of love, we see reflected the qualities that belong to the character of God Himself. God would be less than Jesus if He were lacking in that which Jesus revealed. The character of God cannot be more than that of Jesus, because Jesus' character has nothing wanting in it. It is impossible for us to conceive a moral ideal beyond that which Jesus set forth. Wilhelm Herrmann has put the position clearly. He has said, "The mind and will of the everlasting God encounter us in the historically active will of this man."

Knowing this consciousness of Jesus and the great motivating principles that guided his life, one can have no hesitation in acknowledging that he is divine, that he truly possessed the nature and the character of God. The heart of man is reverent and subdued in his presence, and it has been truly said: "When once he has attracted us by the beauty of His person, and made us bow before Him by His exalted character, then even amidst our deepest doubts the person of Jesus will remain present with us as a thing incomparable, the most precious fact in history, the most precious fact that our life contains."

These facts about the founder of Christianity make it clear why he has always been considered a unique personality. Other religious leaders like Siddhartha Gautama and Mahomet have partially expressed something of the life of God, but no one except Jesus had brought a completely satisfying revelation of Him. It is also understandable how Jesus could be considered by some as existing eternally, for the spirit manifested in his historic person is the eternal character of God Himself.

But some one may conclude that to think of Jesus in the manner described in this chapter makes him no different from other men, who may be divine also. This is partially true, but the difference between the divinity of Jesus and other good souls is one of degree and not one of kind. The grain of sand is infinitely less than the stars in heaven, but both represent chemical elements. The tiny globule of water is like the ocean, but they are not the same. So man possesses divinity, just as Jesus possessed divinity, but we are far removed from the fullness of his life. To move toward that goal should be the Christian's constant desire. We do not drag Jesus down by such an understanding of him, but we lift man to his rightful place as a son of God. We also destroy that dualism which separates man from God and ignores the divine unity which is to be found in Him.

Should We Pray to Jesus?

The prayers of the Christian should always be directed to God. Any disposition to offer our petitions to Jesus himself is apt to create a dualistic

conception of deity, which is contrary to Jesus'
teaching and to the whole insistence of the Christian church even in the period of its theological
controversies. But, we may very properly pray to
God "for Jesus' sake" and "In His name." In so
doing, we express the desire of our hearts to be
identified with him and his purposes and to reflect
his spirit.

CHAPTER VIII

Is God Three Persons in One?

No MORE bewildering conception has ever been introduced into the field of Christian thought than the idea that God is three persons in One. The theological formulation of this belief is known as the doctrine of the Trinity. Although presenting an apparent contradiction in terms and a conception of existence quite beyond the bounds of human experience, this dogma has persisted, vigorously defended by some, bitterly assailed by others, but holding its ground against all opposition for sixteen hundred years. Some theological opinions have commended themselves to one period in the history of the church and have been rejected in another; this tenet has avoided such a fate and is still considered so important in Catholic circles and among some Protestants that it is a vital test of orthodoxy.

But how can one of anything be three of anything? One apple cannot be three apples; one pound cannot be three pounds; one man cannot be three men. Since a person is a unity, how can one God be three persons in One? Understanding breaks down when we try to comprehend a triplicity of being, and even when we turn to the great scholars of the church for light, we get little assistance. Often the belief is simply affirmed without any explanation. Under such circumstances it is not to be expected that the ordinary man, untrained in theological studies, will have a satisfactory comprehension of the Trinity or be able to fathom its meaning. Some devout persons feeling unequal to the task of systematizing Christian thought are willing to accept the authority of the church in this matter. Others give assent because they have been taught from childhood to believe that God is three in one. They do not attempt to defend their position intellectually nor does it play an important part in their religious life. A considerable number repudiate the notion altogether as an essential denial of the unity of God. College men and women have dismissed it as an empty superstition, a formula of ancient ecclesiastics, unworthy of support and furnishing one more reason for indifference to the teachings of Christianity and the church. The reader will have no difficulty in placing himself in one of these categories.

The human mind is so constituted that it seeks an understanding of everything. Primitive peoples are dominated by superstitions and fears but, as man has grown in intelligence, he has struggled constantly to rise above the mysteries and to solve the riddle of existence. This explains all scientific advance and all true achievement. But if God gave man intelligence He intended that man should use it in the field of religion as well as in all other lines of thought. So the modern man is not satisfied to believe in a Trinity which is a mystery; he wants an explanation.

One confusing aspect of the problem for those Christians who look upon the Bible as their final authority, is the absence of the word "Trinity" from the sacred Scriptures. Since the Trinity is a Christian doctrine one does not expect to find mention of it in the Old Testament, but the New Testament makes no reference to it either. Advocates of three persons in one God have insisted that the Old Testament contains suggestions of it. One writer maintains that the book of Genesis presages the Trinity in the use of the words "Jehovah," "angel of Jehovah" and "spirit of Jehovah" and asserts that there is an intimation of it in the triple words in the song of the seraphim, "Holy, holy, holy is the Lord of hosts. The whole earth is full of His glory." Such a position is so obviously strained in support of a predetermined theory, and does such violence to the intelligent use of the Bible, that it need not be given serious consideration. But why did Jesus make no reference to it and why did Paul and the other writers overlook it? Of course it will be recognized that despite this absence of direct allusion or any specific use of the word "Trinity," there are passages in the New Testament that furnish germ ideas from which the belief has developed. The New Testament is permeated with references to God, Christ, and the Holy Spirit, and in two places, at least, these three are definitely linked together. The baptismal formula in Matthew 28:19 reads "Go ye, therefore, and make disciples of all nations baptizing them into the name of the Father and of the Son and of the Holy Spirit," and in Paul's apostolic benediction to the members of the Corinthian church are the words "The grace of the Lord Jesus Christ and the love of God and the communion of the Holy Spirit be with you all." But even these passages do not affirm three persons in one God such as the doctrine of the Trinity has taught.

The first Christian writings in which reference is actually made to the Trinity are the works of Tertullian, an able scholar of the early church who died in 220 A. D. In one passage he states: "The mystery of the economy is still guarded which distributes unity into a Trinity, placing in their order the three persons, the Father, the Son and the Holy Ghost—He is one God from whom these degrees and aspects and forms are reckoned." Two noteworthy facts should be observed regarding this quotation. First, it was written two hundred years after Christ had completed his earthly ministry, a length of time which we can appreciate only by a comparison with the present. Two hundred years back from the present would take us to a period considerably earlier than the Revolutionary War. One wonders why a doctrine that waited so long to put in its appearance should ever have appeared at all. Had the church found something which Christ had not taught, which the disciples did not know, and which the thought of six generations had not revealed? Apparently this was the case. The second observation on Tertullian's words is that he considers the belief a mystery. That point should not be forgotten; it is very significant as subsequent developments will show.

Origin of the Doctrine of the Trinity

The primitive community of believers who constituted the Christian church were Jews, steeped in the traditions and the beliefs of the Semites. The greatest tenet of the Jewish religion was a belief in one God. With clear and unmistakable words the Law had proclaimed, "Hear, O Israel, the Lord our God is *one*"; such was the teaching and such the faith. Greece, Rome, Egypt and Babylon had worshipped many deities, but Semitic thought showed a deeper insight and discerned an essential unity behind all things. Humanity will forever be indebted to the Jews for this contribution of monotheism to a pagan world. Because of this background, a belief in one God was the confidence of the first devotees of the Christian religion. But they felt that their religious experience out-reached the teachings of the Law and the prophets for they had been touched by the life of Jesus. His message had exerted a mighty power over them, their hearts glowed under the subtle influence of his personality, and they were sure he was God's own Son, the long awaited Messiah, who had come at last. But even more had happened for, after Christ had left the world, they were conscious of a new life within themselves. God was dwelling in their hearts, guiding them, sustaining them and bringing them an inward peace. Their leader had promised that this would happen and his words were true.

It was not long before followers in the new cause multiplied, and as the church began to grow it was necessary to defend the faith in a pagan world. In the presentation of their apologetic, as theologians call it, the early Christians were not primarily interested in setting forth an elaborate system of religious thought; indeed, they had not formulated such a system. Such things did not trouble them; it was sufficient that they had found the good life of God revealed in Christ and had felt God's Spirit working in their hearts. But as time went on, the need for a "defense" program was lessened, and then it was a natural sequence that they should attempt to organize their religious thought and to clarify their intellectual positions. They had found God in the universe, in Christ, and in his Holy Spirit; how could this be made clear? At this point the transition occurred whereby attention turned from their experience of God to an effort to expound Him in metaphysical terms.

The real origin for the doctrine of the Trinity is to be found in the attempt to explain Jesus in terms of the Logos theory. This popular philosophical conception has been discussed in another chapter and need not be considered here; however, it should be pointed out that the members of the early Christian church were so convinced that they had found God in Christ, and that he had come from God, that it was an easy step to identify him with the eternal Logos in which the Greeks believed—the emanation of God responsible for the world and the expression of the divine life. The next logical step in the movement of their thought was also to include the Holy Spirit in a full explanation of the Being of the Godhead.

But it is not to be concluded that by following the Greek lead all the difficulties of religious thought were completely and satisfactorily settled. While Jesus was considered the expression of the divine Reason manifested in creation, did it follow that he had existed with God eternally or was there ever a time when he did not exist? Did the

Holy Spirit proceed from God and Christ or from God alone? The Eastern church was particularly concerned with this point. It was never able to reach a satisfactory agreement concerning the Spirit and, finding it difficult to liberate its thought from a certain feeling of subordination in Christ and the Spirit, it insisted that the Spirit proceeded from God alone. It must be said in defense of the Western church that its position represented the more logical conclusion on the basis of the premises, since, if God and Jesus were absolutely identical, it would follow that the Spirit proceeded from both of them and not from God alone. Under the influence of the great Augustine this position prevailed in the Roman church, but East and West were never able to compromise their differences over this metaphysical distinction.

In all this process of establishing a philosophical interpretation of a deep and genuine religious experience, there were quarrels and bickerings marked with deepest acrimony, and peace has never prevailed even until now. When one contemplates the endless confusion of thought, the tragic divisions in Christendom, the hindrance to faith for many good people which arose from theological speculations of men who lived sixteen hundred years ago, he may rightfully inquire whether anything was really gained by attempting to go beyond the experience which comforted, strengthened and sustained the early church for two hundred years, and whether it would not have been wiser to try to bring men to that same experience than to seek their allegiance to a doctrine about it.

The Great Pronouncements

Creeds are the formulas in which experiences are embalmed, and the two great symbols of Christendom in which the belief in the Trinity are preserved are the Nicene and Athanasian creeds. Both of these are acknowledged by the Roman Catholic church today, but the Protestant church does not give them the same authority. The Nicene creed was formulated in 325 A. D., and was probably developed from an old baptismal formula. The statement was re-affirmed at the Council of Constantinople in 381, and put in the form in which it is now used at the Council of Toledo in 589 A. D. The Athanasian creed contains a fuller statement than the earlier document. There are manuscripts of this creed dating back to the eighth century, but the formulation itself goes back two centuries earlier. Its words are stately and imposing: "We worship one God in Trinity, and Trinity in unity, neither confounding the persons nor dividing the substance. For there is one person of the Father, another of the Son, another of the Holy Spirit, but the Godhead of the Father and of the Son and of the Holy Spirit is one, the glory equal, the majesty co-eternal. In this Trinity there is nothing before or after, nothing greater or less, but the whole three Persons are co-eternal together and co-equal, so that in all things as has been said above both the unity in Trinity and the Trinity in unity is to be worshipped." While one holds in reverence and respect all who find comfort and help in this affirmation, it must be frankly admitted that for many persons such a multiplicity of words is bewildering and offers no great help to faith.

Proponents and Opponents

Among the most vigorous champions of the idea of three persons in one God was Augustine, whose position as an original thinker and a leader in ecclesiastical matters is preëminent in the history of the Christian church. Augustine found himself completely at a loss to explain this dogma in all its implications, and frankly acknowledged his limitation in explaining what the creed had stated. In his masterful work on the Trinity, he writes, "There is but one substance or essence and when we speak of three persons it is only because we lack words to express the distinction. Certainly there are three, and yet when it is asked, what three, human language labors from great poverty of speech. We say three persons, not that it may so be said, but that we may not keep silence." In his recognition of this metaphysical statement as a mystery which the mind cannot explain he is taking the same position that Tertullian took over one hundred years before. While the dogma has had generous support all through the church's history, it has been promulgated as a statement of faith and not as a logically established truth.

In so far as logic has been used to support this teaching of the creeds, it has been primarily based upon analogies from life which furnish points of comparison. These are set forth in almost all outlines of Christian doctrine. For example, man is a physical organism and yet has an intellectual life, and a moral life, so there is a way in which the totality of his being may be considered as a triad. Augustine noted that man has a mind, that the mind has an understanding of itself and also a love for itself, thus giving a triplicity in unity. The most important philosophical comparison was the interpretation of Georg Wilhelm Friedrich Hegel, the German philosopher, who felt that the Trinity was an excellent theological statement of his own metaphysical conception of the nature of ultimate reality. All of these speculative ideas and others similar to them have the common weakness of analogies and must be recognized simply as suggestions of likeness rather than convincing proof. They are ingenious, but they do not reach to-day the heart of the common man who, if he knows them at all, only vaguely comprehends their meaning.

Among the outstanding opponents, only a few need to be mentioned. One of the first was a churchman from Ptolemais in Africa, Sabellius by name, whose thought gave rise to the religious movement known as Sabellianism. He insisted that Father, Son, and Spirit were to be considered primarily as manifestations. The leader of the opposition when the Nicene creed was under discussion was Arius, the Libyan, whose failure to conform to the accepted and traditional beliefs of his time caused him an endless amount of trouble. A Protestant protest of a much later date was led by Laelius Socinus and his nephew, Faustus Socinus, Italian theologians of the sixteenth century. Socinianism, named for these two energetic men, maintained the position that God was one, that Christ was a man and the Holy Spirit was the energy of God. The modern Unitarian movement in America found its rise in the eighteenth century and was a revolt against Calvinistic theology. The movement produced a number of leaders of outstanding abilities and some of notable spiritual power. Their efforts were directed against an interpretation of the Trinity that was tantamount to a tri-theism which gave Christians three gods instead of one. Unitarianism represents such a wide range of opinion within its ranks that it is exceedingly difficult to formulate a statement that expresses the Unitarian position as a whole.

The Three Persons

Any historical consideration of the doctrine of the Trinity should take into consideration the use of the word "persons" in this statement of faith. The Greek word used for "person" was *upostasis* and conveyed the idea of substance or essence more than the thought of a personality such as we have to-day. Dr. William Adams Brown, to whom the writer freely acknowledges his indebtedness in the preparation of this chapter, has explained that the Latin word *persona,* which is the translation of the same idea, came originally from the word meaning "mask" and was connected with the old presentation of the drama when masks were used by a single person to present different parts. Thus the "person" was the underlying unity behind the distinctions. One man might play three parts but would not thereby be three distinct centers of conscious thought. According to Dr. Brown, "person," as used in connection with the Trinity, "means a principle of individuation or distinction (as distinct from personification) ." This is a very important point, for much of the confusion which has arisen in modern minds is based upon our failure to grasp the meaning which the writers of the creeds sought to convey and our tendency to think rather of persons as three separate individuals, each one of which has an individual consciousness and will.

A Position for the Modern Man

A recapitulation of the ideas already presented brings to the front certain important considerations which should help the man of to-day reach a satisfactory intellectual position regarding the possibility of three persons being united in one God. They may be set forth as follows:

(1) The doctrine of the Trinity was the outgrowth of a deep and sincere religious experience which its formulators sought to interpret in philosophical terms harmonizing with the prevailing thought forms of their time. For two hundred years the church lived without it, although the process that ultimately brought it into being was going on during that time.

(2) Whatever else we think, we must acknowledge that there is only one God and His life is a unity. This was the position of the Old Testament writers, the New Testament writers and of Jesus himself. Both the champions and the opponents of the Trinitarian formula have zealously insisted that God is one and have strenuously resisted any thought that there are three Gods instead of One.

(3) The Trinity is a purely philosophical idea and its champions have affirmed it to be a doctrine beyond the power of man's mind to explain and one to be accepted on faith.

(4) We cannot maintain that God is three persons in one in the way in which we think of persons to-day—that is, as separate and distinct personalities. To do this would be to set up three gods, and that position has been repudiated with equal fervor by those who have supported the doctrine and those who have repudiated it altogether. Any one who claims that God is three persons, in the modern sense, has neither the Bible nor the Fathers of the church to support his position. He stands alone for an idea which the church has never accepted.

(5) There is a real danger that a continued use of the term, particularly with the different meaning now given to "person," will lead to tritheism, and it may also obscure the humanity of Jesus, which is very essential for a full appreciation of his life to-day. Even the stalwart defenders of Trinitarianism have always maintained that Jesus was human as well as divine, and have bitterly opposed those who ignore this fact. At one time there developed a movement known as docetism, which so stressed the divine element in the life of Jesus that it boldly asserted that a human Jesus did not hang upon the Cross, and that the pain and suffering which he endured did not actually occur but only seemed to occur. This made a deception of the whole tragic drama of Calvary. Trinitarians have ever opposed such a travesty of Jesus' sufferings.

(6) There is one way in which the Trinity may be accepted which is sometimes called the "Trinity of experience." The modern man who follows this belief goes back to the disciples and the early church. The first Christians recognized the God in whom they put their trust as One who manifested Himself in creation, in the life of Jesus and in the movement of God's spirit in their lives. If one has such an experience of God he has all that is vital in the traditional doctrine and all that its writers sought to interpret. It is real as Christ is real and as the Holy Spirit is real. It is as plain as life itself. For those who accept the Scriptures as the final guide of their lives, it is the only Trinity set forth in the Bible.

(7) It may seriously be questioned whether it is advisable even to use the word "Trinity" today. It is a formula of metaphysicians of the past and, according to their own testimony, it is outside the pale of understanding. It is capable of misunderstanding and adds nothing to the meaning of God or the significance of Christ and his Spirit.

Is This Unitarianism?

Someone is likely to claim that any omission of the word "Trinity" from the language of Christian faith is an acknowledgement of Unitarianism. Trinitarianism and Unitarianism are misleading terms of only an historic and academic interest, and they may properly be discarded in our present efforts to understand the Christian religion. In a sense, all Christians are Unitarians in their insistence on the oneness of God. Likewise, practically all Christians are Trinitarians in their recognition that God's life is to be found in Christ and in the movement of his spirit in the hearts of men. In its historical development, the Unitarian movement rendered a real service, which even conservative thinkers have been willing to acknowledge, in its insistence on the oneness of God at a time when many were virtually supporting tri-theism. But modern Unitarianism is difficult to define. It includes some who would deny God altogether or, if not denying Him, at least conceive His Being in such abstract terms as to be of little help to man in his struggle for the good life. Others are primarily humanists, and while humanism sounds a valuable note it does not furnish the dynamic for life by which man may realize his aims. Still others claim that the only way to describe Jesus is to call him human, and in so doing they neither acknowledge his uniqueness nor exalt the divine qualities of his soul. Unitarianism has also tended so to stress God's deity and man's humanity that it creates a popular impression that there is a gulf between man and God. Because of the vagueness of the Unitarian movement, it would be unfair to identify anyone with it simply because that person does not find it necessary to use a third century philosophical concept in order to interpret his Christian faith. We may share the experience of the worthy writers of the creeds even though we do not share their interpretation. The only Trinity that can really help is the one that recognizes that the eternal God is to be found in Christ and acknowledges His presence in the life of the world. This was the only Trinity the apostles knew, the only Trinity that the Bible reveals, the only Trinity that really matters.

CHAPTER IX

What Is Sin and How Do We Get Rid of It?

SIN is a short and ugly word. It is seldom used in
ordinary conversation, and when we wish to convey the idea which it expresses we seek a synonym.
There is a certain inelegance about this subject
which makes us turn away from it very much as
we would recoil from the miasmic odors of a
swamp or the tragic details of human suffering.
Yet sin has played an important part in religion.
It has furnished the basis for grave theological
discussions and for acrimonious debates; elaborate schemes of salvation have been evolved to
get rid of it, and it has led to such vehement expressions of bigotry and intolerance that many
persons have actually sinned in defending the
reality of sin or trying to determine what it is.
There are significant reasons for the large place
which this topic has filled in Christian theology.
First, man has thought of his eternal destiny as
definitely related to his attitude toward sin. If one
follows the right course he may enjoy the bliss of
heaven, but if he moves in the wrong direction

he may be cast into the pit of hell. A second reason is the commonly accepted belief that Jesus'
life is to be interpreted primarily in terms of its
relation to man's salvation.

Two facts stand out in bold opposition to each
other in Christian thought. One is that God is
pure and holy, and every form of evil is contrary
to His moral nature. The other is that man is
weak and sinful, and often chooses a course
directly opposite to the purposes of God. The Jews
not only held to a monotheistic conception of
God, but also surrounded deity with a distinction
of sanctity. This was quite a different notion from
that of contemporary religions in the days of the
prophets. Greek and Roman deities were strikingly lacking in moral perfection, and among the
Canaanites and other primitive groups immoral
practices were a part of the religious rites performed for their gods. The Hebrews, however,
considered their God "of too pure eyes to behold
evil" and Isaiah reflected their thought perfectly
in his prophetic vision, when he described the
seraphim about the throne of God crying one to
another and saying: "Holy, Holy, Holy is Jehovah
of hosts: the whole earth is full of His glory."

Christianity, an outgrowth of Judaism, has continued to emphasize this idea of holiness. Although the early religious life of the Semites revealed a strong devotion to ceremonials and to sacrifice, the message of the prophets was distinctly in favor of righteousness as far more acceptable to Jehovah than perfunctory religious rites. Christians believe that God expects men to seek moral perfection. The clear and unmistakable teaching of Jesus is that God desires that every person shall live a good life and that moral values are of eternal significance. The spirit of the Gospel is reflected in the first general Epistle of Peter, where it is said: "As He who called you is holy, be ye yourselves also holy, because it is written, ye shall be holy for I am holy."

What Is Sin?

The life of man clearly reveals that he has freeaom of choice in determining his own will. As Dante has said:

"Supreme of gifts which God, creating, gave
Of his free bounty; sign most evident
Of goodness, and in His account most prized
Was liberty of will."

With this extraordinary capacity to determine his own course, man faces the tragic possibility of

choosing the evil rather than the good, and yet it
is only when the opportunity for evil is present
that he may achieve moral character. Thus, sin is
best understood as an attitude of the moral will.
It is the definitely determined choice to do that
which is destructive and harmful to the individual or to society rather than that which is uplifting and helpful. It is impossible to get away from
this awful fact of life. A person who sins acts
clearly in opposition to the best in life. He is out
of adjustment with the purposes of God since his
attitude is one of determined opposition to God's
will. Any purposeful lack of conformity on the
part of man's will to that will must bear this
stigma. The person who gives himself over to in-
temperance or excess, thereby breaking down the
physical body which God has given him to express
himself in a material world, is guilty of sin. A
life that is marked by selfishness, malice, bitterness or hate, has the mark of the beast upon it.
Sins robs homes of happiness, fills prisons and peni-
tentiaries, blights social relations, causes racial
hatreds and national antipathies, and destroys the
peace and order of God's universe. Some assert
that sin has no reality, but if we admit the reality
of one kind of moral choice, namely the choice of

the good, we must also acknowledge the reality of the other kind of choice, namely the choice of that which is evil.

Naturally, sin is a relative term and varies with each individual. The little child that unwittingly takes the toy of another child is not to be classed with the thief who robs a bank. The mistakes of the ignorant savage who has low moral standards are not in the same category with those of an enlightened and intelligent man. Increased knowledge means increased moral responsibility, but even in the simplest persons the distinctions between right and wrong are present. The more we understand the mind of God the closer will we approach to an ultimate standard of right and wrong.

The problem now confronting us is to determine how man may get sin out of his life and so make himself acceptable to a holy God.

The Jewish Idea

The Jews were conscious of the problem of sin and worked out a solution in their annual Day of Atonement, which was the time when the national iniquities were removed and the people were brought once more into proper relations with

God. The High Priest acted alone in behalf of all the people. For seven days he kept himself apart from everyone in order to assure his own holiness. Then, after the performance of his regular ceremonial practices in colored robes, he donned white robes, symbolic of purity, and proceeded with clearly defined ceremonial acts. First, he offered a sacrifice for himself and his own family, then one for the sanctuary and finally one for all the people. To make this atonement he entered into the very presence of God in the Holy of Holies. In making the sacrifice for the people, two goats were purchased from public funds and presented at the door of the tabernacle. A lot was cast, and one goat was selected for Jehovah and the other for Azazel. The one for Jehovah was ceremonially slain and its blood sprinkled before the Mercy seat. The High Priest then laid his hands on the goat designated for Azazel and, after the sins of the people were confessed over it, the animal was led away into the wilderness to die. By this colorful ceremony the Jews felt that they got rid of their sins and were brought once more into purity and freedom.

It should be especially observed that in the ceremony of Atonement the blood of the animal was shed in the sacrifice, because this feature had great weight in the development of later thought. But the shedding of blood did not occur because it was thought that there was any special efficacy in blood itself, but because life was considered to be in the blood, and the rite meant that the life of the nation was fully given to God (Cf. Genesis 9:4; Lev. 17:11). It should also be noted that in the minds of the Jews there was no thought that the sacrifice appeased or propitiated the wrath of God. Such is the consensus of opinion of both Jewish and Christian scholars in their interpretation of the Jewish sacrificial system. An understanding of this Jewish idea of reconciliation helps greatly in a knowledge and an interpretation of the Christian conception.

The early followers of Jesus felt that in some way he was an important factor in the adjustment between sinful man and holy God. Their lives had been changed by him, base and ignoble motives had been replaced by good ones and a new and better order had expressed itself. The experience of changed lives through contact with Christ has been true with all his followers, and this fact must not be forgotten. But after men have had a religious experience they are apt to formulate and interpret it in doctrines. All dogmas and creeds are simply the verbal statements of personal experience. But in the case of the Atonement, as in many others, the experience has often been given a wrong interpretation.

The Ransom Theory

One of the earliest theories concerning the way in which God and man are brought into friendly relations with each other is known as the ransom theory of the Atonement, an idea which persisted in the church for over a thousand years and is held by many even to-day. It has been held that as a result of sin man came under the domination of Satan, the spirit of evil, who thus gained control over his soul. In order to get rid of this domination a ransom had to be paid to Satan as a price of release, much as kidnappers in our modern world insist upon a payment for the return of their unfortunate victim. Jesus Christ was the Son of God and Satan desired control over him, so Christ was paid by God to Satan for man's misdeeds and man was restored once more to the Father. Incidentally, Satan made a bad bargain, for while he could control man, he was not strong enough to retain his power over Christ. Thus Christ was free and man also saved from his sin.

This theory has many patent weaknesses. First, it creates a dualism in ultimate reality in that it presupposes a God of goodness and also a god of evil. It suggests that Satan had a right to man which God was bound to recognize. The scheme also implies the suffering of the innocent for the guilty, which is manifestly unfair. By demanding an injustice to Jesus it makes one wrong a substitute for others. It is also based upon a clear fraud worked upon Satan in making a bargain which would clearly result in his defeat. It is strange that these moral inconsistencies and the crass materialism of the whole conception did not impress the early believers. Yet this plan, taught by both Irenaeus and Origen, not only found acceptance in their own time but persisted for centuries.

The Transaction Theory

The second great plan dealing with man's deliverance from sin was advanced by Anselm, the Italian Archbishop of Canterbury who lived in the eleventh century. He promulgated the transaction theory of the Atonement. It was repugnant to his thought that God should render homage to Satan, and he formulated a new idea of Jesus' place in man's salvation. He said that man had sinned against God, and since God was infinite, man was guilty of an infinite sin. The only restitution that could be made for such a sin was infinite restitution, and man himself is unable to make such an offering. But the infinite Son who was himself sinless could make infinite restitution for infinite wrong and thus satisfy God's demand for justice. While this novel conception was free from some of the weaknesses of the ransom theory of Irenaeus and Origen, it had defects of its own. The Bible does not teach that God had to have satisfaction, and yet this thought is basic in Anselm's plan. The same objection also remains that was raised regarding the ransom theory, namely, that wrong may be righted by bestowing punishment on the innocent.

The Legalistic Theory

The legalistic theory derives its name from the analogy it offers to a legal system and a court of law. Plainly stated, it affirms that man, by the commission of sin, violated the law of God, and any violation of law requires punishment. God insists upon the payment of a penalty, and the penalty is death and the pains of hell. In the face of this unfortunate situation, a substitute offered himself at the bar of justice to take man's place, no other than the Son of God himself. He was deemed a worthy sacrifice, so the punishment was inflicted upon him and by his generous act the whole human race was freed from condemnation. All that is required is acceptance of this free gift.

The chief objection to this scheme lies in the character of God, who is portrayed as a harsh, unrelenting deity, who jealously insists upon being given satisfaction to appease his displeasure. We revolt against such a statement as was made by one who defended this position when he said that "Jesus wiped away the red anger spot from the brow of God." The quality of forgiveness is wholly lacking since, by the payment of the penalty, the full obligation of the law is met and man's deliverance belongs to him by right and not through any mercy or divine favor.

The Governmental Theory

A fourth interesting "scheme of salvation" was

advocated by Hugo Grotius, Dutch jurist and theologian. In his opinion God is engaged in the operation of a moral government, and man had done Him an injustice by his sin. It would have been beneath the dignity of such a God simply to forgive man without any demonstration of His displeasure, and such a course would bring His government into contempt. Therefore, God allowed His own Son to be crucified as an example to sinful men of the death which rightfully belonged to them. Thus men are able to see how God hates sin. In this plan Jesus is a symbol and example to all men of the way a moral government feels toward human wrong-doing.

This theory, like the others, is weak in that it involves the innocent suffering for the guilty. It is doubtful whether a sinner would be turned from the error of his ways with only the example of a good man, unfairly treated, as an inspiration to keep him from wrong. The plan of Grotius emphasizes simply the physical death of Jesus, without proper consideration of the moral and spiritual qualities of the innocent victim who willingly accepted the Cross in devotion to his ideals.

The Shedding of Blood

Important in all of these plans was the thought that in some way the blood of Jesus was efficacious in making salvation possible. One can readily understand how this idea of blood atonement came to the front when one recalls the Jewish background of Christianity. It was only natural that parallels and comparisons should have been found with the ancient sacrificial system, but unfortunately Christian thought has given the shedding of the blood quite a different meaning from that which it had in the old Jewish ceremonials. As has been indicated before, the Semites considered the blood simply as an expression of the giving of life, whereas Christian theology has made it of magical significance. Many clergymen have held that the salvation of men would not have been possible if Jesus had not actually poured out blood from his veins as he hung upon the Cross. Such a belief is crass and materialistic and does violence to the Scriptures. It is difficult to understand how God could have found any satisfaction simply by having a few drops of a watery chemical compound drawn from the pain-racked body of the suffering Jesus, and could have ignored that consecration and devotion of the spirit which brought him to his untimely end. If the actual spilling of blood were required, then the soldiers who pierced his hands and feet were true benefactors of the whole human race for, by their nefarious act, they made possible the salvation of all men.

The traditional theories of salvation show a sharp variation from the Jewish sacrificial idea in that they involve a thought quite foreign to the old system, namely, that the innocent had to suffer for the guilty. The animals sacrificed on the altar of the sanctuary were not selected because of their moral innocence, for moral attributes were not considered as belonging to the lower forms of creation, but simply that a clearly understood symbol of the giving of life might be vividly set before the people.

A Modern Theory of Atonement

The average person living to-day has no great interest in the theological ideas of men who lived hundreds of years ago. The opinions of such Ante-Nicene Fathers as Origen and Irenaeus, or the elaborate schemes of Anselm, Abelard, or Grotius, may have an academic interest for theologians but they are far removed from the concerns of the business man of the twentieth century. In fact, it is safe to say that many present-day church-goers have not even heard of these worthy religious gentlemen. But if others, in times past, have had a right to formulate their ideas about the way man can get rid of his sin, why have we not an equal right to do so in the light of our own experience and in accordance with our own highest intelligence? Our problem is to get rid of the sordidness which besmirches our own lives and destroys the happiness of others. We will do well to forget old established systems and such theological words as "satisfaction," "propitiation," "substitution," and "atonement" and try to think through the problem for ourselves.

First, it seems reasonable that salvation is not dependent upon anything being done to change the attitude of God toward man. It is not consistent with an ethical God to believe that He loved man, then came to hate him, and then had to have His wrath appeased by a bloody sacrifice in order again to feel kindly toward man. The attitude of God is one of unchanging love for all His children, as the Bible has clearly indicated, and if any change occurs it must be in a new attitude on the part of man himself. Paul had put the truth correctly: "God was in Christ reconciling the world unto Himself."

The historic Jesus has created a new point of view in human hearts. In this sense the experience of the present coincides with that of the past. The life of Jesus was one of transcendent love. It was a love that did not vanish in the face of hardship or bitter persecution. It was faithful when friends were not faithful. It was a love so relentless and compelling that it took him to the summit of Golgotha and made him the center of the world tragedy enacted there. Here was self-giving devotion that portrays fully and completely the attitude of God toward man. Not only did Christ reveal himself in love but he showed us in his own bitter experiences the extent to which the wickedness and evil purposes of man can go. The sin of man was able to take One completely free from all wrong and deserving of nothing but good and heap upon him contumely, hatred, persecution and bitter physical suffering, and then was cruel enough to pierce his noble body and leave him a withered and blighted thing on Calvary. One cannot view the heart-rending tragedy of the life of this good Man without realizing the ugliness and bestial brutality of the sinful attitude of mind.

One cannot look upon the fullness of that noble Life without understanding the value, the beauty, and abiding worth of goodness. Jesus makes clear the awfulness of wrong-doing and, by the compelling power of his own personality, makes us wish to be like him.

But the final determination whether man shall be freed of sin rests with the individual. The constant unchanging love of God will continue forever. The majestic drama of Christ's own life will ever be before us, with its constant reminder of the extent to which loving sacrifice will go, with its grim portrayal of the hideousness of man's wrong-doing, and with its sublime appeal to live the virtuous life and do the will of God. How will man respond? If we are really impressed by Christ, we will have a true sense of repentance, which is the first requisite for any one who is to turn the course of his life from the evil to the good. God is close to the heart of any person who has reached that attitude of mind. "The Lord is nigh unto them that are of a broken heart and saveth such as be of a contrite spirit." When once man has repented of his misdeeds, he is ready to direct the course of his will toward God. Every time he determines to follow God's purposes for him and does so, he is saved from sin, the sin of just the opposite course. Salvation is thus not simply a single decision made once and for all, but it is a continual process going on during our entire lives. The first decision to do God's will and to follow Christ may be the most momentous one; it may be marked with a deep emotional experience that is never forgotten; but the conflict must always go on, in every moral situation that faces us. It is not sufficient for a person simply to believe that Christ lived and died to help him be delivered from sin; but that faith must be supported by action. As James has said: "Faith without works is dead."

Conceived in this simple way, salvation does not rest upon an elaborate theory of atonement set forth in terms of human bargaining, in the judicial language of a law court or in the phrases of governmental administration. It involves a genuine repentance for sin, a faith in Jesus Christ as the One who has showed the way to God, and a daily determination to follow him. If one will build life on his matchless teachings and fashion character after his noble life, he will do right and not wrong, will choose goodness and not evil and will be continuously saved from sin. All else is subordinate to the determined purpose to give allegiance to that great and supernal Spirit who revealed in his own incomparable character the infinitude of the love of God.

Is There Such a Thing as Original Sin?

The early Fathers of the church held that Adam voluntarily violated the commandment of God and, as the result of his wrong-doing, sin was passed on to the whole human race. Augustine held that human nature existed completely in Adam, and by his transgression all men became corrupted. Anselm agreed with this point of view and felt that both body and soul were tainted by Adam's fall. In the Council of Trent the Roman Catholic church supported the doctrine, but held that by baptism the guilt of original sin is removed. This idea of original sin has persisted through the Reformers and down even to the present day, but despite the place given to it in Catholic and Protestant doctrine, it is not one to which the modern man can give assent. It is now generally recognized that the human race did not descend from initial parents brought into full creation by a fiat of God, but that man has developed from lower to higher forms of life through God's slow and laborious processes of evolution.

The story of Creation in the book of Genesis is simply a pious and reverent attempt on the part of an ancient people to explain the mystery of creation. It was formulated at a time when science had not developed, and should be considered not as historical fact but as poetry in which is revealed a rare spiritual insight. This theory of original sin is unacceptable because it is contrary to every conception of justice. It would be unfair for all human souls to be cursed by the mistake of a single person, and it offends our sensibilities to feel that a child dying in infancy should be eternally shut off from the life of God by virtue of such sin. Doubtless the belief developed through a recognition of the social forms of sin which are difficult to allocate to individuals. But the most reasonable conception of sin is to interpret it primarily as an individual matter where each one is to blame in accordance with his own personal choices.

Can an Individual Be Saved from Sin After Death?

A commonly-accepted theory of the past has been that the salvation available for man through Jesus Christ must be accepted now, in this earthly

life, or else the offender will be lost forever. But
such a position is not tenable, if God is just. Many
persons with unfortunate hereditary antecedents
and with bad social environment are hindered in
their discovery of God and the goodness that is to
be found in Christ. One has only to contemplate
the poverty of great cities, the tragedies of broken
homes, the evil influences of corrupt surround-
ings, to realize the inequalities of life and of opportunity which many are compelled to face. It is
inconceivable that God would love us and seek to
reclaim us as His own until the day of our death
and then lose all further interest in us. Human
love is not like that. Rather, we must believe that
He will continue to reach out for us here and
hereafter, ever bidding us to do His will. Since
man is a free moral agent, there will always be the
tragic possibility that he may not respond to that
appeal. So long as he refuses to do so, the destructive power of his sin will continue to rob his life
of its fullest possibilities and will bring its devastating social consequences to the lives of others.

CHAPTER X

What May We Believe about Miracles?

BEFORE we formulate any judgment regarding the miracles of the Bible we should have clearly in our mind what is meant by this mooted term. There are two methods which have been used in the interpretation of human experience, namely the natural and the supernatural. The natural is the usual or customary procedure in the life of the universe. For example, the planets move in their orbits with immutable regularity; water congeals at 32° Fahrenheit and changes into vapor at 212° Fahrenheit; the seasons follow each other with unvarying sequence. Man has been examining the customary operations of the physical universe for a long time, and out of these observations has formulated natural laws. He has reached the conclusion that given the same conditions the results will always be identical. If there should ever be a single deviation from the operation of a so-called natural law, the scientist at once would relegate the formulation to the scrap heap of fallacy and error. Such a preponderance of evidence

has been adduced in favor of the absolute reliability of nature that men trust it completely. Elaborate systems of science have been developed on
this assumption, and human beings build bridges,
skyscrapers, locomotives and steamships with complete assurance that the laws of the physical world
will always remain the same.

But some persons believe that occasional incidents occur which are outside the natural operation of law, and these unusual happenings are considered supernatural. A supernatural event is
looked upon as an intrusion into nature's customary procedure, in which the ordinary laws of the
universe are momentarily suspended and something occurs which is in direct violation to them.

The average person is very apt to associate a
miracle with the supernatural. He considers that
God has suspended his usual process in order to
achieve some desired end. Thomas Aquinas reflected this point of view in his assertion that a
miracle is something outside of nature, and Leib-
nitz, corroborating this same position, affirmed
that the laws of nature are not necessary and eternal, and God can suspend them for his own purposes if He so desires.

But is it necessary that a miracle should be interpreted as a supernatural event contradictory to the laws of the universe? Certainly such an idea could not have been in the mind of the ancient Jews and the early Christians for the simple reason that they knew nothing about science and had formulated no laws for the interpretation of their world. To the contemporaries of the Biblical writers, a miracle was simply an unexplained sign or wonder which attracted attention by its unusual character. Therefore, we do violence to a correct understanding of these events if we hold the idea that those who reported them construed them to be an interruption of laws, since they knew absolutely nothing about such systematic classifications.

It should be recognized that although miracles do not involve a contradiction of natural law they might have to do with facts outside of the present limits of our understanding of natural processes. There is more about the world that we do not know than our present knowledge has revealed, and each day brings some fresh insights into its mystery and wonder. Immanuel Kant, the great German philosopher, believed in natural law and yet stood for the possibility of miracles as actual events, because he believed such phenomena might be altogether in accord with laws that we do not know. We have many modern evidences of facts that would have been interpreted miraculously a few generations ago. An X-ray machine would have been a miracle in the days of the Revolution, and an automobile, an airplane or a radio would have been put in the same category. Yet these modern inventions function in accordance with clearly-defined natural laws, and have no semblance of mystery to-day.

Any adequate conception of God requires that we recognize His ability to interfere in the ordinary operations of the natural world if He so desires—otherwise the mechanism would be greater than the Creator which produced it. But no phenomenon of nature could be considered unnatural to Him. When rare phenomena occur, we should not discard them simply because they are rare, but should examine all the evidence related to them and adjust our scientific formulations to include them. The scientific man always follows this procedure.

Our Attitude toward Miracles

There are many people who would gladly dismiss all miracles from the Bible as events altogether outside the realm of probability, and would think of them simply as erroneous tradition or misrepresented fact. They believe that in so doing the ethical and spiritual content of the Scriptures stand out more clearly and helpfully. It is their contention that any attempt to accept miracles at face value tends to destroy confidence in the Bible itself, and thus detracts from the spiritual power which this great Book should rightfully exert. These sincere seekers for Truth feel that miracles add nothing to our appreciation of God or our understanding of Jesus Christ, and hold that if Christ subordinated miracles in his ministry, and would not allow his reputation to be established on their validity, we should not give them a more important consideration.

There are others who hold a directly antithetical position. They contend that miracles furnish irrefutable testimony to the power of God and to the place which Christ was intended to fill in the divine plan, so that to deny their reality would be tantamount to a complete invalidation of the trustworthiness of the Scriptures. They argue that there is nothing unreasonable in the thought that God should occasionally interfere with his regular methods of operation for some definite purpose, and some feel that He does so even to-day. Only recently a New England woman insisted that she talked every night with her deceased husband through the medium of a ouija board, and was guided by what he advised her to do. There is nothing inconsistent in such a belief if one accepts the major premise that God does act supernaturally from time to time.

The quasi-scientific person is not disposed to accept anything outside of the realm of the demonstrable, and yet this is hardly the true scientific attitude. The uniformity of law on which science builds its structure is a definite assumption in itself and there is no absolute assurance that the laws which are recognized to-day will be operative a thousand years hence. The proper attitude toward miracles is not to accept them with a blind faith, nor to deny them with equal dogmatic assurance, but to weigh all the evidence in each given instance and to formulate conclusions on the basis of all observations. The best science can do is to assert that miracles conceived as interventions in the natural world are highly improbable. The overwhelming evidence from the book of nature and from painstaking studies in many branches of human knowledge supports the position that this is a rational and intelligible universe completely controlled by laws established for man's good, and that these laws are themselves a testimony of God's love for man. As Browning says:

"I have gone the whole round of creation: I saw
    and I spoke . . .
 I spoke as I saw:
 I report, as a man may of God's work—
 All's love, yet all's law."

Such a universe is infinitely more reliable and trustworthy than a capricious one. This should be the position of likeliest probability, of most reasonable presumption, with which to approach the miracles of the Bible.

General Observations Regarding Biblical Miracles

Even the most casual student would not be disposed to accept all miracles of the Bible with the same degree of credulity, and particularly would make a distinction between Old Testament and New Testament miracles. There are fifty recorded miracles in the ancient Jewish Scriptures, and these include such spectacular incidents as the ten plagues visited upon the Egyptians (Exodus, 7, 8, 9, 10, 12, 14), the staying of the sun by

Joshua (Joshua 10:12-14), the destruction of mocking children (II Kings 2:24), the floating iron ax-head (II Kings 6:5-7), and many others equally amazing. The miracles of the Old Testament are much further back in history than the events in the Christian tradition, and naturally the evidence for them is much less trustworthy. It was very common for ancient peoples to believe in the miraculous, as the history of other religions clearly indicates, and primitive-minded persons would accept such notions readily. Many of the Old Testament miracles are related to control over the material universe and have nothing to do with physical healing, while New Testament miracles deal largely with restoration of physical bodies, and center in the exercise of power by Jesus himself.

The principle of motive should always be considered in our appraisal of miracles. If God performed the miracles attributed to Him in the Bible He must have had some definite purpose in each particular case. It will be observed that in a number of the miracles in the Old Testament the motive involved is not particularly significant. God did not have to perform miracles to demonstrate His power, and if He sought to convince men of His greatness, He could have accomplished the same result through the persuasive powers of prophet and seer without performing mysterious phenomena to startle them into belief.

Miracles Associated with Folk-Lore

There are some miracles in the Bible, particularly in the Old Testament, that are easily recognized as folk-lore and are so bizarre that a modern person could not possibly accept them as established fact. The story of Balaam's ass (Numbers 22:21ff) furnishes a striking illustration. The ass saw an angel of the Lord, which his master did not observe, standing in the way, and so turned aside to avoid it. The lowly animal pushed Balaam's foot against a wall, severely injuring it, and the irate master punished his faithful beast. Whereupon the animal started a conversation with Balaam and talked with him about his cruelty. Then Balaam's eyes were opened and he, too, saw the angel and forthwith repented of his action. Such a miracle requires a belief in angels capable of being visible or invisible at will, and also demands faith in the ability of an animal to use the language of human beings. Such a fantas-

tic event places altogether too great a strain on
credulity to find ready acceptance.

A second miracle of this type is connected with
Hezekiah, and occurred when he was grievously
ill (Isaiah 38:1ff). The Lord agreed to restore
Hezekiah, and this promise should have been sufficient assurance for any one, but to prove that he
would keep His word He caused the shadow on
the sun dial of Ahaz to go back ten degrees. Such
an act suggests not only a disturbance of the whole
solar system, but brings a serious reflection on the
trustworthiness of God Himself.

The floating of the iron ax-head at the word of
the prophet Elisha recorded in II Kings 6:6ff reveals a demonstration of supernatural power not
by God directly but by an ordinary man who enjoyed the divine favor. The friends of the prophet
had determined to build him a house, and one of
the workmen engaged in this laudable enterprise
accidently dropped his ax into the water. This
was especially disturbing to the zealous but unfortunate workman for the ax was a borrowed one.
But he appealed to the good prophet in his trouble, and Elisha hewed down a stick, cast it into
the water, and the iron ax-head magically ap-

peared floating on the water and was easily rescued.

Miracles of the types indicated are so naïve, and have such insignificant motives behind them, that the intelligent man dismisses them at once as imaginative tales believed by primitive peoples regarding great and outstanding persons who have had the respect and veneration of their race.

Miracles Arising from a Misunderstanding

There are some events which have been placed in the category of the miraculous through a definite misunderstanding of the facts. When Joshua made his famous attack against the Amorites (Joshua 10:12ff) he longed for the complete destruction of the enemy. In order to accomplish this bloody purpose he prayed for the sun to stand still that the day might be prolonged and his foes be utterly destroyed, and God answered this request exactly in accordance with his desires. This narrative is now understood in an entirely different and much more reasonable way. The record indicates that Joshua may have been seeking to inspire his soldiers as he was leading them to battle, and so quoted a poem from the ancient Book of Jashar in which God commanded the sun to stand still in order that victory might be more complete, and this poetic quotation, written in the imagery and suggestiveness of poetry, has been accepted by practical minded individuals as a narration of actual fact.

A similar type of miracle is one in the New Testament associated with the Gerasene demoniac (Mark 5:1-15). This unfortunate man, according to the thought of his time, was possessed with devils, although we now know that he was insane. When Jesus proposed to cast out these devils, they besought him that they might go into a herd of swine near by, a particularly appropriate place for evil spirits in the minds of Jewish people, who looked upon pork as unclean. Jesus gave this permission, and as the devils came out of the man, writhing and twisting on the ground, the swine stampeded into the sea and were drowned. The circumstances in this case may have been quite natural. It is altogether conceivable that this man of deranged mind in the paroxysms of his affliction started a stampede of swine near by, and that these animals rushed blindly into the water. It is plausible to believe that Jesus brought peace and serenity of mind to this troubled man through the confidence and strength which his own noble personality created, and the emotional outburst and the subsequent onrushing of the swine were natural incidents, later elaborated into the idea of a miraculous event.

Normal Events Miraculously Interpreted

Closely associated with the miracles based upon incorrect interpretation of the facts are those which represent perfectly normal events which were conceived as miraculous. The parting of the Red Sea (Exodus 14:21-31) might have happened through the power of a strong east wind which pushed back the waters and permitted the Hebrew children to pass safely across a shallow part. The death of Uzzah (II Samuel 6:6ff), resulting from his well-meaning effort to steady the ark of the Lord which he feared would fall from the unsteady cart, may have been an unusual coincidence, like sudden death from heart failure, or possibly the result of shock which came to the unfortunate man with the thought that he had laid hands on the sacred dwelling place of God Himself. Similarly, the burning of the sacrifice on Mt. Carmel (I Kings: 18-25ff) may have come about through a fortuitous stroke of lightning from the heavens.

It may be proper, by way of interpolation, to refer to a miracle associated with an extra-biblical character, which is exceedingly well known, and comes under this very classification. This is the miracle of the stigmata of St. Francis of Assisi. It has been commonly held that St. Francis meditated so much upon the life of his Lord and the tragedy of his crucifixion that there was reproduced on his own body the nail-prints in the hands and feet of Jesus. A physician named Dr. Edward Hartung has made a study of the physical ailments of St. Francis on the basis of all available evidence and has interpreted his illness in the light of modern scientific knowledge. He has discovered that St. Francis was afflicted with malaria of the quartan type, which caused him much suffering and made him the victim of chills every fourth day during the latter part of his life. One of the symptoms found occasionally in this type of malaria is hemorrhage of the blood in the skin, which causes large purple spots on the body. These show usually in the hands and feet and "appear as ovoid bluish, at times slightly elevated spots." If Dr. Hartung is correct, the stigmata of St. Francis were quite normal, although unusual, and a commonly-accepted miracle finds an altogether normal interpretation.

Miracles Associated with Rare Phenomena

Some miracles are probably nothing more than rare phenomena which have been given a miraculous interpretation. Matthew records the finding of a coin in a fish's mouth which Peter used to pay the temple tax (Matthew 17:27-47). Many rare objects have been found in the entrails of fish, and a coin could have been found in this case. Some think that Jesus may have instructed Peter to catch a fish, sell it and use the money to pay this tax. The stilling of the tempest by Jesus (Mark 4:35-41) may have been associated with a perfectly normal event, for the sea of Galilee is subject even to-day to storms which agitate the waters greatly and subside as quickly as they appear. Something Jesus may have said at such a time may have become connected in the minds of the disciples with such an incident, and a miracle resulted. Another event which may be considered as in the category of natural but unusual phenomena is the miraculous draught of fishes (Luke 5:1-11). It is much more satisfactory to believe that an unusually large school of fishes happened to find their way into the disciples' snare than to think that Jesus exercised a power of magic which caused these creatures of the sea to enmesh themselves in the disciples' nets. An emotionally enthusiastic group of followers could easily have given a miraculous interpretation to this event.

Miracles Associated with Control of the World of Nature

There are seven miracles associated with Jesus which are definitely related to control over the world of nature as contrasted with control over human life. Three of these are the miracles associated with rare phenomena to which reference has already been made, and the four others are the withering of the fig tree (Mark 11:12-14—20-25), the walking on the sea (Mark 6:45-52), the feeding of the five thousand (Mark 6:39ff) and the miracle of changing water into wine at the wedding feast, a miracle recorded by John alone (John 2:1-11). If we are to think of Jesus as belonging to the realm of humans so far as his physical life is concerned and not in possession of all the attributes of God, a limitation which he himself acknowledged, it is impossible to hold to any conception of a supernatural power over nature. But these miracles have reasonably clear explanations. The cursing of the fig tree occurred at a time when the tree had no fruit upon it, and it is a strange incongruity that the wrath of Jesus should have been directed against a tree that was simply following the normal laws of growth. This miracle should be associated with the parable of the fig tree which the owner had intended to cut down but which the vine-dresser sought to save by proper fertilization and care. It has been thought that the parable may be linked to Jesus' visit to Jerusalem, which is the fig tree of the narrative, and the rejection of Jesus by the Jews, represented by the withering of the tree. A parable of this type could easily have been changed through the processes of oral tradition from a helpful story to an unusual miracle.

The walking of Jesus on the sea (Mark 6:45-52) has been given many interpretations, some of which are as difficult to comprehend as the miracle itself. The story involves an act of levitation on the part of Jesus which neutralized the normal pull of gravitation. It seems most likely that, in this instance, an allegorical event has been changed into a record of historical fact. One interesting hypothesis is related to the events in the life of Jesus after his resurrection. The disciples were embarked on troubled waters without their leader, although they were expecting to see him at the second coming. Suddenly he appears before them on the troubled waters of life, walking with ease and assurance. He enters the boat of the church and all is well. This interpretation by J. M. Thompson in his *Miracles in the New Testament* is a plausible, rationalistic explanation of an event which, if conceived in actual reality, presents many difficulties to the scientifically-minded man.

The miracle of the feeding of the five thousand is the only one recorded in all four gospels. There is another record of feeding of four thousand reported in Mark and Matthew (Mark 8:1-9, Matthew 15:32-39) which is clearly a duplicate narrative excepting that the number of persons involved is smaller. Innumerable efforts have been made to explain this miracle on purely rational grounds, but the most plausible is an interpretation of the miracle which links it with the Eucharist. In that great sacrament it was felt that Jesus spiritually fed the faithful and there was always enough to meet the needs of those who came, no matter how many there were. Gradually this idea of providing for the spiritual wants of his followers came to be given this materialistic and miraculous interpretation.

The changing of water into wine has always been a stumbling block to those who have sought a reasonable explanation for the actions of Jesus. This miracle occurred through no spoken command or without any contact with the wine itself. Servants poured out the wine simply at the command of Jesus. The record suggests that there is symbolical significance to be attached to the act, as John's gospel is written with a definitely spiritual rather than an historical purpose. The story suggests some radical change accomplished through the power of Jesus, possibly a transformation of man's nature from the natural to the divine or, as Pfleiderer has intimated, the substitution of the new truth which Christ brought for the old Law of the past. Interpreted symbolically, the story teaches a vital and powerful truth; interpreted as a record of real fact it calls for control over natural elements and chemical changes wholly outside the bounds of probability or plausibility.

Miracles Associated with the Raising of the Dead

The Old Testament gives some record of the dead brought to life by miraculous intervention, as in the case of the widow's son restored by Elijah (I Kings 17:17ff) or the dead man cast into the sepulchre of Elisha, who became alive simply by touching the prophet's bones (II Kings 13:21). But the ones which most engage our attention are the three miracles of this type attributed to Jesus, namely, the resurrection of Jairus' daughter (Mark 5:21-24), the resuscitation of the son of the widow of Nain recorded by Luke alone (Luke 7:11-17), and the raising of Lazarus (John 11: 1-46). It is quite certain that actual death did not occur in any of these instances. In the case of Jairus' daughter, we have Jesus' own testimony that she was not dead, but simply asleep (Cf. Mark 5:29). The possibility of a cataleptic trance or state of coma must be recognized in the case of the widow of Nain's son, and also of Lazarus. Medical diagnosis was not so highly developed in Biblical times as it is to-day, and we know that even in modern times medical records tell of cases where apparent death was not death at all. In oriental countries the dead were buried quickly on account of the hot climate and also the religious beliefs of the people, so that often there must have been too hasty judgment and action in such cases. It is well known that in the gospel of John, which is a devotional interpretation of the thought of Jesus, there is a frequent tendency to heighten the details of an incident for definitely spiritual purposes. This does not mean that this gospel furnishes an inaccurate portrayal of the life of Jesus, but simply that it should be interpreted in light of the clear purpose of the author. A heightening of details is apparent in the record regarding Lazarus.

Miracles of Faith and of Definite Healing

The interpretation of the miracles of Jesus rationalistically does not mean that no healings actually occurred; on the contrary, even after eliminating the miracles which have been reasonably explained in other ways, there is evidence that Jesus accomplished many actual cures. Modern psychiatrists know that physical states are closely related to mental states, and even such afflictions as deafness, paralysis, and blindness may be superinduced by mental conditions. Jesus called on those whom he helped to exercise faith, and he frequently said: "Thy faith hath made thee whole." When the disciples asked him why they were unable to effect a healing, he replied: "Because of your unbelief." Jesus not only sought the mental attitude of hopeful expectancy on the part of the individuals that he served, but he endeavored to enlist an attitude of trust and confidence in the minds of others who were interested.

In cases attributed to demoniacal possession, one can readily understand how the calm, confident spirit of Jesus could allay hysteria and establish serenity of mind. Medical science is familiar with paralysis of bodily functions due to disturbed mental states, and the case of the paralytic carried upon the litter (Mark 2:3) or the man with the withered hand (Mark 3:1), furnish Biblical parallels. The healing of the woman who suffered from an issue of blood (Mark 5:25), the restoration of St. Peter's wife's mother (Matthew 8:14), and even the healing of the leper (Mark 1:40) — there are various kinds of leprosy—may be classified as faith healings. In one instance at least, namely, in the case of the blind man (John 9:6), Jesus used a common therapeutic method of the time in anointing the parts of the afflicted victim with spittle. There are a considerable number of miracles of healing performed by Jesus that find striking parallels in the field of modern psychotherapy. Carpenter's *Mental Physiology*, or Du-Bois' *Psychic Treatment of Nervous Disorders*, furnish interesting and illuminating evidence of the power of changed mental attitudes to effect cures. There is no more reason why we should deny the reality of miracles of this type resulting from the calm contagious influence which radiated from the soul of Jesus than we would repudiate the results of modern scientific efforts in the mental treatment of nervous and functional disorders.

Facts to Be Remembered

When we interpret the miracles of the Bible on the basis followed in this presentation, we should remember that these conclusions rest upon considerations of intrinsic probability. All our difficulties are not solved by such an interpretation, but even if we hold to the possibility of God's power being expressed in intervention of the laws of nature, we must decide whether it is more likely that he would follow such a course or hold himself inerrantly to his eternal expression of love in a law-controlled universe. To give miracles a super-natural explanation creates more problems that to interpret them on a rationalistic basis.

All religions reveal a miraculous element in them, and this is particularly characteristic of the faith of simple primitive people of deep emotional nature. This readily explains the recorded miracles of the Old Testament. In the course of the Christian religion, the early information regarding Jesus was transferred first by oral tradition, and even the earliest gospel of Mark was not written until thirty or forty years after Jesus' death. In such a period of time it would be very easy for narratives to become heightened in detail, natural events to be interpreted as supernatural, or parabolic expressions given a touch of reality. It seems highly improbable that God should have interfered with the operation of the universe in order to accomplish specific results through supernatural means in the cases of the few incidents recorded in the Scriptures, and not carry out a similar process in the subsequent passing of time. Certainly Jesus did not seek or desire to build his reputation upon miraculous achievements.

A true Christian life and an honest Christian experience do not depend on a literal acceptance of all Biblical miracles. Jesus subordinated the idea of the miraculous in his experiences in the wilderness, and surely his followers should grant them no more important place than he gave to them. Someone has said that a life might be as full of miracles as that of Jesus and still have little spiritual significance, and at the same time we could remove the miracles from the life of Jesus and he would still be the world's greatest spiritual authority. God does not need the unnatural in order to make Himself known, for He has revealed Himself in all the processes of law, in the beauty and wonder of the physical universe, in the life of man, and supremely in the life of Jesus himself. If we do not believe in miracles, we do not have to deny God. Probably the most reasonable conclusion is that a number of events occurred in the life of Jesus which the people of his time could not explain, but these involved no contradiction of the laws of nature, although they may have been in accordance with laws which were not understood and which we do not even now clearly comprehend. However, we should not be afraid to be honest with ourselves, and if our faith cannot accept the possibility of miracles we should be frank to acknowledge it. Meanwhile, it is not reasonable to believe that God is indifferent toward any of his children simply because they find their faith in miracles overcast by a cloud of uncertainty.

CHAPTER XI

Is It Worth While to Pray?

IF THIS question were presented to any considerable group of people there would be many con-
flicting answers. The following illustrations from
the writer's personal experience are typical. An
aged man told this brief and simple story out of
his life. He had been brought to the very gates of
death by pneumonia, and it was not thought that
he could survive. On the morning after the crisis,
when the physician entered the sick room, he said
to the patient: "I did not expect to find you here
to-day." Whereupon the stricken man replied:
"Well, doctor, you do not deserve credit for this.
I want you to know that the people of my church
were praying for me, and God Almighty has raised
me up." No power under heaven could shake this
man's sure conviction that prayer had saved him.

Contrast this reaction with another point of
view presented by two Christian women. Said
one: "I no longer pray. I don't feel like praying.
Even in my recent sorrow I did not pray for the
member of my family who was sick." And the

other woman added: "I believe that ninety-five per cent of the people who pray have no idea that their prayers will be answered." Who is right? Was the old gentleman cherishing the comforting assurance of a delusion, or were the alert young women deceived by the superficial reasoning of a cynical skepticism?

Prayer has been defined in many ways. Some think of it as a hope, an aspiration or a longing. This sentiment is reflected in the words of James Montgomery's hymn "Prayer is the soul's sincere desire, uttered or unexpressed." Others call it "The reverent outreach of the soul toward God." Likewise, it may be described as "a conversation with God," which may take the form, on our part, of the spoken word, or simply the formulated thought of the mind. While all definitions are valuable, for our present purposes let us think of prayer in this particular way; namely, as a conversation, a communication of ideas between God and man. I realize that this definition is very incomplete. It would not receive a very high mark in a class in theology, but it comes fairly close to what the average person means by prayer. This is what a child does when he prays at his mother's knee. It is what the minister does in the pulpit on Sunday. It is .what the anxious parent does when serious illness threatens a member of the household.

The honest man will admit that, with our present knowledge, it is not possible to answer every question about prayer and meet every intellectual difficulty. Some of the deepest realities of life are shrouded in eternal mystery. What we can do is to recognize that prayer plays an important part in the religious life of man, inquire what is its value and discover how it may best be understood.

As a preliminary observation, it may be noted that all through history prayer has played an important part in the religious life of the race. The Vedic hymns of the Hindus are among the oldest religious literature in the world, and these contain prayers of supplication to the great forces of nature. The Jewish religion is permeated with prayer, and the uplifting influences of the Psalms in the Jewish hymn book are still felt in the life of the world. The Indians whom Columbus discovered on the shores of America had a religious life that involved the exercise of prayer. The devout Buddhist spends hours in mystic contemplation, and the Mohammedan uses prayer five times each day in his devotions. Prayer has played an important part in the Catholic and Protestant churches, and has a place in every service of worship. Of course, if there is no value to such an act, then the human race has been engaged in a futile exercise for centuries. On the other hand, a strong presumption is created by this universal practice that prayer does something for us that is distinctly worth while.

In times of imminent danger or grave emergency we turn instinctively to God in prayer. We do not ask reasoned arguments for belief, we are not concerned with intellectual difficulties, we do not examine our own worthiness to ask a favor of God. We simply pray, saint and sinner alike, that help may be given us in our hour of need. One may reasonably believe that such instinctive action is helpful to us, just as other similar reactions are helpful. The instinct of fear stimulates us to alertness and action. The instinct for self-preservation causes us to resist the forces that would destroy us. Therefore, it is rational to believe that genuine benefits are also derived from the practice of prayer.

Some Prayers Present No Intellectual Difficulties

Our conversations with God may take the form of simple communion with Him, and in this respect may be much like a visit with a friend. When we call at the home of a neighbor we do not usually go to ask a favor. We visit him because we enjoy his company and find pleasure in talking over matters of common interest. If our friend happens to be a person of position and eminence, an authority in some field of knowledge, we go away inspired by our contact with him and our conversations are particularly helpful. But if such personal associations are beneficial, how much greater should be the benefits of conversation with God. When we seek Him we reach out toward the center of all Life and Energy, toward the source of all Truth and Power, toward the Will and Purpose of the universe. If one is face to face with the inexorable forces of the world, or hard against the adamantine rock of stern reality, it means something to feel that God is near. In His presence we may pour out our joys and our sorrows, our enthusiasms and our perplexities, our aspirations and our defeats.

Of course, a conversation is never one-sided,

and God always has something to say to man. The Quakers and the followers of the Oxford movement, wisely recognizing the importance of silence and meditation in prayer, feel that the periods of quiet are as truly a part of their devotions as their own spoken word. When God speaks to us in prayer he does not actually talk in the English language, but he responds exactly as the neighbor does when we visit him. He brings the impact and the influence of His whole personality to bear upon us so that we become keenly aware of Him. Whenever one contemplates the supreme Order of the universe, the eternal values of beauty, goodness and truth, the Personal Will that is at the heart of all things, a strong integrating force asserts itself within him. There is a new appraisal of values, a consciousness of power, a reënforcement of wavering purpose. In the prayer of communion we sense the infinite Purpose that is expressing itself all about us, and which is striving to assert itself in our lives also. At such a time, our experience transcends description; in such a place we stand on holy ground, for God Himself is there. No one could doubt the tremendous value of this kind of prayer in the life of anyone who consistently and regularly practices it.

Prayer may likewise take the form of thanksgiving, a simple expression of gratitude for the blessings of life. Life has many sorrows, and the pain and travail of the world is everywhere evident; in poverty, in sickness and in the defeated hopes and thwarted ambitions of men. But there is still much left for which we may be grateful. We have the same beautiful world, with its endless variety, its changing seasons, its perpetual fascination. We have home and friends, love and loyalty, health and freedom, literature and art, church and state. We have not lost the joy of achievement, nor the thrill of noble unselfishness. These sources of happiness and of deep satisfaction must come from somewhere. They can come only from the Creator of all things, from the bountiful hand of God. A person would be sorely lacking in the finer sensibilities of life who would not express the gratitude of his heart to a friend for a kindness shown or a favor done. It is a pathetic picture which the Bible portrays of ten lepers cleansed by Christ, and only one thoughtful enough to return thanks. Prayer is a medium of courtesy. To thank God for His blessings is not simply an acknowledgment of favors received; it is an act which preserves our self-respect and offers an opportunity for the development and culture of the soul.

The average person has no intellectual difficulties with the prayer of communion or thanksgiving. He would readily admit the value of such prayer, and would acknowledge the propriety of it, but asks many questions about prayers of petition. He wants to know whether God will do anything for him if he prays which would not be done if he does not pray. Is it justifiable to believe in prayer in a world of law? Is it proper to impose our wishes on a God who already knows what is best for us?

Some Prayers Will Not Be Answered

If we were to make a careful examination of the requests which we make of God in prayer, the results would be illuminating. There are some prayers which, if answered, would actually bring us harm. If every small boy who wanted a real gun and asked for it in prayer should have gained his desired end, the number of youthful fatalities would have been greatly increased. Some of our prayers are very selfish and do not take into consideration the rights of others in God's great family. The owner of a worthless farm might pray to have an old state road changed so that it would pass through his property and enhance its values, but the garage men and small merchants, who had established themselves on the old road and who had invested their life savings in their properties, might be greatly damaged if such a course were followed. Some prayers create an impossible situation for God. In a city voting on a bond issue for public schools, the parents whose children would be benefited thereby might ask God to carry the election their way, but other citizens who had no children and wished to keep down the tax rate might request just the opposite. Army officers are assigned from time to time to different headquarters. Such an officer might well pray that he could be assigned to a definite post in a distant location which would be interesting and adventurous to him, while his mother-in-law might pray that his assignment might be nearer home so that she could see her daughter more frequently. We had a good illustration of the impossibility of God answering all prayers during the late war, when the German people asked for victory and the Allies did the same.

If prayer could produce anything we want simply by asking for it, it would make every man a

magician and we would have a topsy-turvy world
with no reliability in it. The lazy man who pre-
ferred not to work could ask for gold and it would
be poured into his hands. The student unwilling
to take time to go to college could pray for the
wisdom of an Edison or an Einstein and the feat
would be accomplished. An aspiring young man
could pray for the favor of his lady's hand, and if
he made his request first, all other suitors would
be out of the competition. The manager of the
baseball park could ask for fair weather in order
to increase his gate receipts, and although the air
might be heavy with moisture and rain might be
sorely needed, the courses of nature would be
directed by his personal inclination.

Some prayers represent a distinct invasion into
the field of natural law. It must be admitted that
it is highly valuable to be able to rely on our universe. There would be no progress, and we could
have no reliance on the future if the world were
not established in this way. The bridge that was
erected to stand a definite strain to-day would be
worthless to-morrow. The fields which produce
their bounty for man one year might be barren
the next and leave us empty-handed. Nothing
would be sure. Of course, our present universe

contains the awful possibility that the individual
may suffer from a violation of law. A man could
scarcely consider himself secure from danger if
he prayed the Lord to keep him from getting hit
by an automobile, and then were utterly careless
in crossing the streets. One could not expose himself to contagious disease and expect immunity by
ignoring prophylactic measures and simply trust-
ing to prayer.

Since God has made clear His loving purpose
by creating a world of law, an abrogation of these
laws in response to our petty requests would suggest that He is a very weak Being, or else, that His
wisdom was so short-sighted that He could easily
be moved to change His original idea. We cannot
expect God to do this simply because of our constant importunity. As Milton has said in "Paradise Lost,"

> "If by prayer
> Incessant I could hope to change the will
> Of Him who all things can, I would not cease
> To weary Him with my assiduous cries:
> But pray'r against His absolute decree
> No more avails than breath against the wind
> Blown stifling back on him that breathes it forth:
> Therefore to His great bidding I submit."

Yet something more needs to be said regarding prayer in its relation to natural law. It has been held by some that a universe of law is so determined that prayer is utterly useless. Of such a world it has been written: "Stern as fate, absolute as tyranny, merciless as death, too vast to praise, too inexorable to propitiate, it has no ear for prayer, no heart of sympathy, no arm to save."

However, the immutability of law does not preclude the possibility of answered prayer, for we do not know all laws. There must be many which we have not yet discovered. Fifty years ago it would have seemed contrary to law to suspend ten tons of dead weight in the atmosphere, but the modern airplane has demonstrated that it is not. It would have seemed lawless for the human voice to be carried around the globe in an instant of time, but now it can be done. God can accomplish what seems impossible in a world of law through the operation of laws not yet known to us. The reign of law must be recognized in our approach to the problems of prayer, but it does not demand that faith in prayer must be surrendered.

Let us admit frankly, then, that prayers will not be answered which will do us harm, which would make us workers of magic, which leave out

of consideration the rights of others and which
are contrary to natural law. However, our considerations have not yet wholly exhausted the field
of human petitions which men bring to their
Heavenly Father, for there are some things that
we desire which do not come under any of the
classifications already indicated, and we should
formulate a judgment about them.

Some Prayers Will Be Answered

It is my firm conviction that God does answer
some of our just and reasonable prayers, and that
He does so in very natural ways, and wholly within
His world of law. One of our difficulties with
prayer is that we think that an answer must come
through a special revelation, in a definite act, or
in a definite period of time. Any answer is "a
response," and whenever God reacts to our moods
of prayer in any way, we are getting a reply from
Him. To make this clear, let me be specific. A
young man is out of work and he prays that he
may find a job. One way God could answer such
a request would be to have a letter arrive in the
next mail offering a position. Probably no such
reply would come. But, as the young man brings
himself into God's presence, he begins to realize

that he is in a friendly world and not an unfriendly one, he becomes aware that he is not an insignificant creation but is a son of God with all the gifts and capacities of one in such a station. New confidence is engendered, self-respect asserts itself, imagination is quickened, possible new approaches to employers occur to him, and out of the renewed spiritual vitality of his contact with God he goes out to secure that which he desires. Surely this would be an answer to prayer more reasonable and justifiable than to expect God to accomplish the result alone. Of course, some one might say that God had nothing to do with such a response, that the result was simply the reflex action of a man's own thoughts. But if there is a God—and such a conviction is inescapable—then the result of such a prayer has its origin in the additional factor introduced into the experience by which the human spirit was quickened.

It is quite possible for a person to pray for one thing and never get the favor that he asks—and yet have the prayer answered in a definite and positive manner. A young man working in a drug store might become interested in pharmacy and pray that the way might open for him to get a training in that field. Yet out of his contact with

God and the meditation of his prayer he might come to realize that he could go farther than the limited scope of that laudable profession and become a physician, ministering to the bodily needs of his fellow-men. In such a case God's answer would be a denial of the original request and yet the prayer would truly be answered.

But one may say to all of this: "I am willing to recognize the possibilities of such an answer to prayer, but is it worth while to pray that a sick child be restored to health? Can a mother whose erring son has run away from home expect to get her son back again through prayer?" To such questions we may reply that the desired results even in such situations are not outside of the range of possibility. In the first instance, the stimulated imagination and insight of prayer might bring to the parent or, by suggestion, to the attending physician, some new method of approach to the child's illness that would effect a recovery. Dean Bosworth of Oberlin used to tell his students that one could believe in intercessory prayer if it is possible for God to put a thought into the mind of man. We know very little about the laws of the mental or psychical realm. They may be as numerous and as powerful as the laws of the physical world. Future generations will certainly know infinitely more about such matters than we do to-day. It is not hard to believe that God could bring to the wayward son an impression from something that was read, or from an address that was heard, or from an observed situation, that would prompt him to recognize his filial responsibilities and cause him to return to the family fireside.

Still another question may be raised. "Since God is infinite in knowledge and love, why should He not be relied upon to do his best for us even though we do not ask him?" Any rational conception of God justifies a belief in his unfailing goodness, but the fact remains that some things cannot be accomplished unless we are ready to coöperate. A field might be able to yield an abundant harvest, but man must till the soil and plant the crops if the results are to be obtained. A sufferer from hay fever might be benefited by high altitudes, but it is necessary to go to the mountains if the proper results are to be obtained. So God is ready and willing to help us, but His assistance will not be available until we ourselves

have the attitude of mind, the understanding and
the stimulation which prayer alone produces.
Prayer brings a renewed awareness of the reality
of God, of the significance of the spiritual world,
of the inherent capacities which we ourselves
possess, and from these very values may come a
realization of that which the heart desires. Untold
blessings await us if we will use the means by
which they come.

The Best Kind of Prayer

The more we cultivate the practice of prayer the
more the human desire will seek to attain the will
of God. We have reached the highest level of
prayer when we are ready to commit ourselves
wholly and unreservedly to Him. At the time
Jesus was passing through the agony of his dark
hour he prayed: "Abba Father, all things are possible unto thee; remove this cup from me! How-
beit, not what I will, but what thou wilt." This is
prayer at its best. The habit of prayer will surely
lead us to this same mental attitude. We will
realize the limitations of our own human judgment, the indefensible folly of many of our requests, and we will seek to know God's will and
purpose for us.

We should not miss the benefits of prayer simply because we cannot explain its working or comprehend its mysteries. The spirit that prompts a person in his need to turn to God for help justifies a confidence in the validity and helpfulness of prayer. We do not know all about electricity, but we take the knowledge that we possess and use it for our advantage. We do not completely understand human personality. Even the members of our own families are only partially comprehended, and although our relations with them are most intimate their real selves are hidden in the arcana of the human soul. But, despite our limitations, we enjoy them and are helped by our contacts with them. So we do not know all about prayer, how it works, why it does not always produce the results we desire. But powerful psychic and spiritual forces are certain to operate when a human personality finds contact with the Life, the spiritual Energy, the Soul that is at the heart of the universe. It is the witness of countless thousands of devout and reverent souls that prayer has been a source of blessing, an inspiration and a comfort, that it has been the means of tapping unrealized sources of power.

Conclusions

Is it worth while to pray? I answer strongly in the affirmative. It brings us fellowship with God, with all the uplift, inspiration and insight which such a relation is certain to produce. It brings the strength of God and the resources of the universe to our assistance. It puts man in the position where God can do His best for him. It offers the possibility that our requests may be granted through laws and influences that we can only partially comprehend. It helps to shape the human will into conformity with the divine purpose behind the universe. The greatest spiritual Seer that humanity has produced, Jesus of Nazareth, believed in prayer and cultivated it. He taught his disciples to pray. His judgment cannot be ignored. A man that prays will be better than one who does not pray. A church that prays will be a powerful and effective organization. A nation that prays will be likely to shape its plans and order its life in harmony with the noblest ideals of humanity. As Tennyson has said, in *The Passing of Arthur:*

"More things are wrought by prayer,
　Than this world dreams of. Wherefore let thy
　voice

Rise like a fountain for me night and day.
For what are men better than sheep or goats,
That nourish a blind life within the brain.
If, knowing God, they lift not hands of prayer,
Both for themselves and those who call them
    friend?
For so the whole round earth is every way
Bound by gold chains about the feet of God."

CHAPTER XII

Is There Life after Death?

THERE is no subject of thought about which the human mind craves certainty with more earnestness than personal immortality. If a man could be found anywhere who, out of his own experience, could furnish absolute and irrefutable proof of the continuance of life after death, the world would make a pathway to his door. As it is, we stand in the presence of a great mystery, baffled and perplexed. A wife, a child, a husband, dearer to us than all the treasures of the world, is taken from us. Our grief is inconsolable and we can hardly endure the devastating loneliness. During the waking hours of the day our loved one is the companion of our constant thought. In the stillness of the night we toss on restless beds until, perhaps lost in fitful sleep, we are startled by some dream which momentarily makes us feel that the one for whom we long is near. Consciousness brings us back to stark reality. We pray! We hope! We cry out in stern rebellion. If only we could know assuredly that the one whom we have lost still lives, and that we would meet again, our minds would rest in peace.

One finds a certain dissatisfaction with the way in which immortality is frequently discussed. The analogy of returning life in nature is not satisfactory. The ancient Romans and Greeks had a time of celebration in the spring for the beauties of the natural world that had come back again. They offered their prayers and their votive offerings to the gods and goddesses who clothed the earth anew in its garment of emerald sheen. But all this is not convincing, for the flower that rises this spring is not the same one that shed its beauty a year ago. It is another blossom altogether. To be sure, there is a comparison in nature in that life continues to take one form after another, but it is only a comparison. We are reminded by others that a parent lives in the life of his offspring, who in turn lives in the life of another, and so the life principle passes on through endless generations. This is genealogical immortality, but it is not the subject in which the average man is really interested. Likewise we know that there is a certain immortality of influence. One person affects another, and their lives are modified to a degree by such a contact, since man is the totality of all his experiences. So influence passes from generation to generation. George Eliot spoke of this sort of immortality when she wrote:

"O may I join the choir invisible
Of those immortal dead who live again
In minds made better by their presence."

Such a thought is impressive and sobering to contemplate, but it does not reach the vital problem of personal immortality.

What man wants to know is whether he will exist as a conscious, continuous self-realizing personality after the processes of physical dissolution, and whether he can know others who have also passed into the mysterious life of the unseen.

Some are certain that we have absolute, experimental proof of immortality. Whatever we may think of the societies for psychical research, absolute candor compels us to admit that many intelligent men . have been identified with them. Sir William Crookes, Sir Oliver Lodge, Alfred Russell Wallace, Camille Flammarion and Dr. William James of Harvard University have such established reputations in the field of science as to lift them above suspicion, so far as personal integrity is concerned. Their observations should be received with open mind. If it should be discovered some day that there are certain persons who, under certain conditions, are able to make contact with the spiritual world through clearly defined natural laws, such a fact would be no more mysterious than the operation of the radio.

We will do well to start our considerations of this important subject with the position that immortality cannot be proved. In order to demonstrate immortality conclusively it would be necessary for us to find a person who had lived eternally, and that is a manifest impossibility. In making the admission that we have no absolute proof for immortality, one must recognize that a denial of immortality cannot be proved either. We do not have the faith of a believer pitted against the fact of the skeptic, but we have the faith of one pitted against the faith of the other, and the intelligent man must decide which faith is the more reasonable. We must weigh dispassionately the testimony of every branch of human knowledge and discover whether these fields of human thought create a preponderance of argument in favor of survival after death or whether they lead to an opposite conclusion. It is my contention that *immortality is not an established fact, but a reasonable hope.*

One Difficulty Removed

Many people have found it hard to believe in personal immortality because they are unable to think of consciousness existent apart from the human brain. When the heart ceases to beat and the blood no longer circulates, human personality apparently ceases to function, and it has been concluded that the mental life is simply an expression of the functions of the brain. However, this is a position which scientists do not hold to-day. Thirty-five years ago John Fiske pointed out in the Ingersoll lectures that consciousness is quite outside of the physical vibrations and activities of the nervous system, and is simply the concomitant state that goes with them. In his interesting book *Brain and Personality*, W. Hanna Thomson, after exhaustive study of the brain and its functions, makes the following positive statement: "We have definitely concluded that the facts both of brain anatomy and of brain physiology indicate that this organ of the personality is never other than its instrument, while the personality itself is as different and as separate from it as the violinist is separate from, and not the product of his violin." There is no proof that conscious activity cannot exist apart from a human organism, for the simple reason that our experience does not reach into such a field. A sponge fastened to a rock in the sea, if it were conscious, would have no knowledge of the realm in which a fish lives, and a fish would have no knowledge of the realm of land creatures, and yet both are realities. Our experience is very limited, and we cannot speak dogmatically regarding that which is beyond it.

It is quite clear that the conscious self is an entity quite apart from the brain and the nervous system. The body may be limited in its functions through physical infirmities, as when one loses an arm or a limb, or in those conditions where certain areas of the brain are atrophied, but the self goes on, fully aware of its own reality. The physical brain is a constantly changing organism, with cells breaking down and new ones constantly replacing them, but the conscious self is an unchanging reality. Man clearly shows a capacity to choose, and to exercise personal freedom which would be quite impossible if the self were merely the expression of changing physical activities in the brain. Many scientists are of the opinion that the physical body and the conscious self are not two different realities, but simply aspects of the same reality. Dr. C. C. Hearst of Cambridge has said in his writing, *The Mechanism of Creative Evolution,* that there seems to be no valid scientific objection to the belief in a future existence in the form of pure thought or spirit. On the testimony of the scientists themselves, we may therefore dismiss the idea which is often held, that it is unscientific to believe that personal consciousness can exist apart from a physical organism.

A Noteworthy Observation

It is significant to observe that all through the development of human history man's highest reasoning has led him to a belief in the great idea of life after death. While there are some groups that have not held to this idea, the literature of antiquity indicates a preponderance of faith in the persistence of the soul after death. It has played a part in the animistic religions, in Buddhism, Mohammedanism, Judaism and Christianity. The belief is so universal as to suggest that it is almost instinctive with us. Why should we not hold that such a persistent idea is a reflection of ultimate truth? Is it conceivable that the minds of so many peoples at all times have philosophized

on life and have reached an utterly fallacious conclusion? It is with the recognition of this point of
view that Addison makes Cato say:

"It must be so, Plato, thou reasonest well,
  Else when this pleasing hope, this fond desire,
      this yearning after immortality?
  Or whence this sacred dread, this inward horror
  Of falling into nought? Why shrinks the soul
  Back on herself and startles at destruction.
  'Tis the divinity that stirs within us,
  'Tis heaven itself that points out a hereafter
      And intimates eternity to man.
      Eternity, thou pleasing, dreadful thought!"

The Witness of Science

Science deals with observed phenomena, and
since immortality is beyond the limits of experience science can furnish no proof for immortality.
But as has already been indicated, science cannot
disprove the continuance of life after death either.
Whatever science may contribute to our problem
arises out of the suggestions of intrinsic probability from known experience. Our observations
of the world process suggests a general scheme of
development from the inorganic to the organic,
and from the organic to the psychical. The climax
of the cosmic process is Man, with all his capaci-

ties for thought, for aspiration and for achievement. This mighty trend creates a strong presumption that man is a valuable creation. Now if
it were true that man is valuable simply as a
creature to live for a few brief decades and then
be destroyed, the age-long development comes to
naught and the universe is meaningless and irra-
tional. This is contrary to all our observations for,
if the natural world reveals anything, it is reason-
ableness and purpose. The whole evolutionary
trend indicates a purpose in the mind of God to
create a being of eternal significance.

Science likewise teaches that matter and energy
are indestructible. No one has ever been able to
annihilate the tiniest atom of matter, and the law
of the conservation of matter is the expression of
that fact. Energy assumes various forms, but continues undiminished. The water turns the dynamo
that produces the electricity which refrigerates
the ice-chest, lights the room or heats the grill,
but it is always the same energy appearing in different form. But there is something more certain
and more real than matter or energy—it is the
spirit, the ego, the soul of man. It is so powerful
that it controls both force and matter. It reaches
out to interpret the cosmos. This is a strange uni-

verse if lesser realities are indestructible and the greatest reality is as fleeting as a burned out taper.

The Demand for Justice

A belief in immortality finds further support in the thought that God could not possibly be just if there is no existence after death. We know that this life does not always deal fairly with men. There are poor people in crowded city slums who have never had a fair chance. There are children born sickly, bearing in their frail bodies the taint and the skin of their progenitors. What opportunity have they had? They have been handicapped from the beginning. There are men who have always done right and yet have always had trouble, while others who have continuously done wrong have flourished like the green bay tree. If God is just, if He is worthy of our worship, there must be a future existence where present wrongs will be adjusted and every human soul will come into its reasonable reward.

Man's Unfulfilled Desires

Likewise our unfulfilled desires cry out for immortality. Man feels the limitations which this earthly life places upon him. He aspires for some-

thing greater, higher, nobler than anything which
he has attained. He lives to grow, to develop, to
achieve, but life places a restricting hand upon
him. Sometimes it is the limitation of physical
infirmity, sometimes the hindrance of economic
want, sometimes sheer lack of time. Death beck-
ons us long before we have obtained our heart's
desires. Thus we find man, the supreme product
of an age-long process of creation, as a being possessing capacities for growth far beyond the
opportunities for earthly realization, and it would
be a strange world if the processes of his development should be cut off abruptly. It would mean
that our dreams, our ambitions and our out-
reaches are but futile errands, and it would make
the earth a paradise of fools. No wonder that one
poetic soul should say:

"If this be all and other life awaits us not,
   Then I say it is a stupid cheat, a wretched
      bungle,
   I for one protest against it,
   And hurl it back with scorn."

The Dignity of Man Himself

One of the strongest presumptions in favor of
immortality is found in the inherent value of

man himself. Man is a little lower than the angels. He is crowned with glory and honor. The cosmic process extended through unnumbered millenia has produced a being with mental capacities capable of comprehending and evaluating the universe itself, divine, Godlike, a creature worthy of an eternal destiny. All of us have had some persons indirectly linked with our lives who have demonstrated in the noble dignity of their conduct the eternal worth of the human soul. Common sense will not permit us to think that such persons are merely dust and ashes. Browning once said: "There is not one lost good." It is infinitely easier to believe that a noble soul lives on with God than to feel that such a one is gone beyond recall. Someone may say that we live for the generation that is to follow. If this is so, and if man is simply a stone upon which another stone may be placed, for what purpose and end is such a building process going on?

One cannot ignore the spiritual supremacy of Jesus in answering this vital question. His life has revealed the potential worth of every human soul. Not only is true value of human character revealed in his historic Person, but his own testimony regarding immortality is worthy of consid-

eration. It is our common practice to seek expert
information from those best fitted by training and
experience to give it. Robert Millikan must be
heard in the field of physics. Sir James Jean and
Sir Arthur Eddington are authoritative sources
in astronomy. If we had a problem in mathematics, we would listen to the opinion of Professor Einstein. In a similar manner we should
seek evidence from authority in the field of
spiritual experience. Of all persons who ever
lived, the historic Jesus of Nazareth is the one
whose judgment we would accept in such deeply
important matters. He had a more intimate contact with God than any person we have ever
known. He lived with God in terms of close fellowship. Jesus believed in a future life as surely as
he believed in the reality of his earthly life. He
spoke of that life with the confidence with which
one might speak of his daily existence. Jesus made
man so important in the sight of God that only
immortality becomes him. Likewise, Jesus gave
man an ideal quite impossible of realization in
the future years at our disposal upon earth. Allow
man eternity, and Jesus' goal for him may be ful-
filled. The representation of life which Jesus
brought to the world cries out for immortality as

the only condition under which that life finds its fullest meaning.

Will We Recognize Others?

My belief that we will recognize others in the spiritual life after the processes of physical disso-lution are over is predicated on the importance of personal relations in our earthly life. The greatest thing in the world is persons, and they are our source of deepest satisfaction. Love and friendship are indispensable requirements of the human soul, and if God were to grant us a future existence in which these supreme values were to be taken from us, he would be giving us an exist-ence which no one would want, and it would deprive us of that which earthly experience has revealed to be most worth while. We cannot think of God as unreasonable or without mercy, and therefore a belief in the continuance of our per-sonal relations after death is wholly justifiable.

Some Speculations

No one knows the nature of that future life, and any convictions which we may have regarding it must necessarily be based on speculation. How-ever, it is natural that we should seek to formulate our notions of what the existence after death may be like on the basis of our earthly life and what experience has brought to us.

There are some who believe that the gift of immortal life will not come to everyone, but only to those whose earthly careers give evidence of promise and of worth. This is sometimes called conditional immortality. It is not a position that is easy of acceptance. Goodness and evil are qualities of the soul which may be acquired in this earthly life, and there is no reason to believe that they cannot be acquired even after the soul is separated from its physical vehicle of expression. For God to cast aside that which has been morally defective during the few brief years which constitute the earthly span, and to ignore the possibilities of change which greater time and larger influence could produce, creates a strange inconsistency. This would be a waste of that which could be of infinite utility. Conditional immortality, involving, as it would, vast numbers of God's children, would represent "the horror of immeasurable failure." The inability of many to attain moral superiority is often due to social conditions over which the individual has had no control, and for which he cannot be held directly responsible. In view of such possibilities, it seems more likely that the love of God will continue to play eternally upon souls that exist eternally and that the potentiality of personal reclamation will abide forever.

The Catholic church maintains that the soul of man is not ready at death to enter the full bliss of heaven and that it is necessary to pass through an intermediate stage known as purgatory. Such an abode is a place to which those go who are not good enough for heaven or bad enough for hell. In this state the erring person endures punishment for his sins, for it is insisted that while God pardons sin He does not agree to remove the penalty. As a corollary of this doctrine, it is taught that while the individual in purgatory can do nothing to change his own condition, it is possible to help him through the prayers and offerings of the living for the dead. Mere money cannot buy these favors, but they come only through the spiritual exercises of the faithful. The belief in purgatory is supported by certain interpretation of Old and New Testament passages, by quotations from the Fathers of the Church and by action of the ecclesiastical councils of Florence (1438-1445) and Trent (1545-1563).

The Protestant church does not follow the Catholic position on this point, but there is an elemental principle involved that is worthy of recognition. It seems reasonable to hold that life in the future will be a continuance of our existence here, and that we will take up our new existence where we have left off in our earthly careers. Personally, I believe that we will not enter the other world in a state of perfection, and that the good man and the murderer, the life-long Christian and the death-bed repentant will not start a celestial career on levels of absolute equality. Our weaknesses and our virtues will go with us and probably we will make mistakes as often as we do on earth.

I believe that we will still possess the power of free choice. Freedom of the will is a noble gift, and if it is necessary for the development of moral character on earth, it must be a requisite for that same result in the heavenly kingdom. With growing knowledge and deeper spiritual insight, however, the drift will be most likely toward a full and complete obedience to the will of God as the best course for the realization of our highest selves. This would suggest that ultimately all will be saved by God, and that salvation is not eternally settled by this earthly life. I feel that man will be disposed eventually to bring himself into harmony with the infinite Will, but the possibility will always remain for a soul eternally to reject God. The Bible speaks of an unpardonable sin, and many unfortunate people have been driven to despair by the thought that they have committed it. The only unpardonable sin is the eternal rejection of the appeal of God and, as the Bible has indicated, an unpardonable sin is an eternal sin. This is not quite the same position as that taken by Universalists, in that the acceptance of God's love will always rest with the individual soul; there will be no compulsions. But it is difficult to see how anyone, after the processes of enlightenment and deeper insight have played upon him, would willfully turn away from God.

How about the earth's unfortunates, sometimes called imbeciles, idiots, morons? Of them we can say that unquestionably their lives are limited in the physical world by the imperfect vehicles through which their personalities have had expression. Necessarily, these personalities have not had the opportunity for advancement which has come to others but, freed from the limitations of impaired bodies, their souls should likewise have opportunities for growth and for fuller expression.

No one can conjecture satisfactorily regarding the body with which the soul may be clothed. The traditional position accepted by the Catholic church is that men "will rise again with their own bodies which they now bear about with them," and this teaching is found in the Apostles', Nicene and Athanasian creeds. Many Protestants hold a similar point of view, basing their contention on selected passages of Scripture which seem to furnish corroborative evidence. I cannot hold to this position. We know that every moment of our lives our physical bodies are changing, and the worn, disease-afflicted body we possess when death overtakes us is apt to be a weak and ineffective instrument. The chemical elements of the body soon return to the earth from whence they came, and re-appear in other forms of created life. If the spiritual realm is not hampered by the limitations of physical existence, a physical body would be of no use there. One ingenious writer, familiar with modern scientific knowledge and the structure of the atom with its inter-ionic spaces, has suggested the possibility that even now we could have spiritual bodies conformable to our present physical ones without any surrender of our present knowledge of cellular structure, and that a spiritual body of such a character could maintain itself after physical dissolution. But we know so little about personality that we might better leave all such speculations to the future. We cannot localize personality now, and localization may be quite unnecessary; the important characteristic of personality is Will, and if that survives, all questions of corporal association with it are secondary.

Conclusion

Now let us summon the witnesses for immortality or against it, before the bar of Reason. No absolute testimony is offered on either side. We must decide whether we will have faith in immortality or faith in the destruction of the human soul. *Science* speaks and says: "My field is with the experimental and the demonstrable, so I cannot furnish positive evidence, but I likewise cannot furnish a scintilla of fact to deny this noble hope; indeed the evolutionary processes and the laws of conservation establish a strong presumption that human personality will be permanent." "*Universal Desire,* what is your testimony?"

And *Universal Desire* replies: "All through history the aspirations of man in his moments of
highest thought have led to this conviction. There
must be a reality corresponding to that which instinctively asserts itself in the human heart!"
"*Justice,* what is your testimony?" And *Justice*
speaks: "I demand it; the instinct for fair play is
rooted deeply in the life of man. Wrong exists,
evils must be corrected, right must triumph, but
the process is slow. It demands time for the realization of justice. Only immortality can satisfy."
"*Common Sense,* what have you to offer?" And
Common Sense insists: "I am guided by practical
thought. I have looked upon the lives of many
and find that in the most depraved there are elements of good. Many souls have a noble dignity
and a sublime work that suggests God Himself.
Many good people have made it clear that they
are worthy of immortal life. Why should God cast
them ruthlessly aside?" "*Religion,* what have you
to say?" And *Religion* speaks: "I bring the strong
assertive faith of Christ himself. He believed in a
future life; his closest friends were convinced of
it. The early Christian church was founded upon
this noble hope. The tomb was not able to re-
strain the Son of Man; the powers of death and

Hell yielded to him as he arose on the first glorious Easter morning to bear witness to the truth." Now, let us have the verdict. "If a man dies, shall he live again?" Answer: He shall live, O glorious thought, he shall live again!